THE SHOOTING OF

JOHN F. KENNEDY

One Assassin

Three Shots, Three Hits — No Misses

THE SHOOTING OF

JOHN F. KENNEDY

One Assassin

Three Shots, Three Hits — No Misses

by Col. WILLIAM H. HANSON, USAF (Ret)

The Naylor Company
Book Publishers of the Southwest
San Antonio, Texas

CONTENTS

v

PREFACE

A President assassinated, shot down with a high powered rifle like a running animal; his alleged assailant murdered, literally executed in the hands of the law by a self-appointed executioner; then the executioner, in turn, cut down by the great mystery killer itself — cancer. All this is irrefutable and needs no further explanation.

The President silenced on the scene; his assailant professing innocence until death; the executioner admitting of no conspiracy though slowly being overtaken by death. All this is essentially irrefutable but seems to require both explanation and correlation.

A Governor caught in the line of fire, grievously wounded, recovered, only to be caught again in the line of questioning — and doubted. This demands explanation.

In the aftermath, a policeman killed because he intercepted the assailant's route of escape. This murder explains itself; it obviously grew out of the other terrible deed.

These acts of violence and death were criminal in the extreme and all needed the test of the law in its due process, but dead men cannot be tried in our courts of law.

Many still like to believe that had the law been able to take its course, the cause of justice would have been properly served, and all circumstances surrounding the assassination, the murders and the wounding would have come out into the light of day. Many, at the time, seemed to sense (and savor) the poetic justice to be seen in the untimely deaths of the alleged assassin and his executioner. Even a few believed that the policeman had died an un- related death.

All were bound to feel that crimes of such magnitude must have had more illustrious or more notorious per- petrators than a lone disturbed young man and a small- time girlie show entrepreneur.

These conjectures can be matched with a hundred others and, even then, they would only serve to point up the monumental task that confronted the President's Com- mission when it set out, as specifically directed: "to ex- amine the evidence developed by the Federal Bureau of In- vestigation and any additional evidence that may hereafter come to light or be uncovered by federal or state authori- ties; to make such further investigation as the Commission finds desirable; to evaluate all the facts and circumstances surrounding such assassination, including the subsequent violent death of the man charged with the assassination, and report to me [President Lyndon B. Johnson] its findings and conclusions."

The Warren Commission, as it came to be called, has long since acted and rendered its report. The public has not been happy with the Warren Report, particularly with its inconclusive findings regarding the paths and effects, and the sequencing, of the three rifle bullets that it cor- rectly determined were fired at the presidential limousine. Its many critics, capitalizing on its inconclusiveness in this critical regard, are still having a field day with the entire report.

There has been a continuing clamor for a reopening of the investigation, but this would be fruitless because, to date, no one has successfully disproved the Commission's allegedly unproven principal conclusion that there was only one assassin who acted alone.

Perhaps a more specific and less encompassing presidential directive was in order at the start, one directing no more than a determination of how the President was killed and how Governor John B. Connally, Jr., was wounded. Then, if such did not determine by whom the President was assassinated, an evaluation of all the surrounding and related circumstances would have been in order.

With such a limited directive, there is little doubt but that a selected group of trained investigators would have readily determined exactly what took place, ballistically and traumatically, during the half-dozen fateful seconds that took the life of our 35th President.

This book should be a refreshing change for the average American, as it makes just such a determination. Using straight-line investigative techniques and with reader participation, it simply unravels the mystery that has surrounded the three rifle bullets fired at the presidential limousine. Specifically, it demonstrates and proves, beyond any question of a doubt, that President Kennedy was struck by all three bullets and that the Governor got caught in the line of fire.

The establishment of these primary facts is shown to give full substantiation to the Commission's principal conclusion that a single assassin, acting alone, fired these three bullets at the President, thereby killing him and inadvertently wounding Governor Connally.

One thing this book does for sure — it drives away all but one of a ghostly band of conspiratorial assassins who have been haunting Dealey Plaza in Dallas, Texas, since the 22nd of November 1963.

Col. William H. Hanson, USAF (Ret)

Part I

ABOUT THIS BOOK

Chapter I

WHY THE STORY?

The author had taken only a casual interest in the activities of the President's Commission prior to the publication of its report in the fall of 1964. The case against the alleged assassin seemed clear enough as reported in the various news releases that had followed the assassination.

Like many others, he assumed that the Commission had done its job thoroughly (and with a minimum of delay) and that the President was only doing his public duty in making its findings and conclusions, and supporting documents, available to the general public.

An authoritative paperback,[1] published in October 1964 by Bantam Books (with the help and advice of the national staff of *The New York Times*), insured wide distribution of the full text of the Commission's Report to the reading public.

Many believed, at the time, that both the President and

3

the Commission wanted the Report widely disseminated, hoping that its exceedingly broad and comprehensive evaluation of the overall circumstances would put the public mind at rest on the matter and close the Government's case against the person then charged with the assassination.

But, as the Scottish poet put it, "The best laid schemes o' mice and men gang aft a-gley." By early 1966, the critics were beginning to be heard; by mid-1966, they were in full cry as were both the defenders and apologists of the Report.

The President's Commission, having promulgated its Report, had necessarily withdrawn into the sanctuary of official silence, leaving its Report to stand (or fall) on its merit.

The author's interest in the developing controversy over the official Report was not renewed until mid-1967 at which time the Associated Press published a special article written by two of its ace staff writers, Sid Moody and Bernard Gavzer, in which a valiant effort was made to stand up for the Commission and its Report against a growing list of critics and disclaimers.

As the Commission, in fact, had failed to properly support its findings and conclusions pertaining to the *shooting episode* of the assassination, the best that these two fine writers could do by way of defending the Report was to offer the general observation that the Commission had supported its conclusions at least as well if not better than the disclaimers were supporting their own theories and derogatory pronouncements.

By and large, the Associated Press did a great service in releasing this series of articles. In the first place, the releases served to enlighten the reading public by pointing up the main differences and disagreements between the official Report and the fast growing number of discreditors. Secondly, it triggered other interested news agencies to go to press, so to speak, and shed what light or comment they could on the issues pointed by Messrs. Moody and Gavzer.

4

The author just happened to tune in on the television program "CBS Inquiry" monitored by the well-known news commentator, Walter Cronkite. This television program highlighted even further the factors in the official Report which, due to their inconclusiveness, had given the more vehement critics and disclaimers a basis for questioning the validity of the entire official Report and a large part of its supporting documentation.

The many references during the above programs and news releases to the Zapruder movie film[2] sent the author to the files to dig out *Life Magazine's* 29 November 1963 issue (Vol. 55, No. 22) with its pictorial coverage of the actual assassination, and its 25 November 1966 issue[3] (Vol. 61, No. 22) which presented selected Zapruder movie film pictures in color.

These color pictures (with blowups) in the 25 November 1966 issue of *Life Magazine* were background for a featured interview with Texas Governor John B. Connally, Jr., covering his own personal analysis of the individual pictures of the Zapruder film strip and his opinion of how they correlated with the eyewitness testimony that he had given to the Commission's interrogators.

It was apparent from the interview that Governor Connally staunchly held to his original testimony — and unshakeable belief — that he had been wounded by the second of three bullets fired at the presidential limousine.

The interview also made it clear that Governor Connally's unshakeable belief that the second bullet had caused his wounds, somehow contravened a theory put forth by one of the Commission's own counsels, Attorney Arlen Specter, that the bullet which had caused Governor Connally's multiple wounds had also caused the President's neck wound.[4]

Whereas the application of the theory required that both

5

men react simultaneously to this single bullet, the Zapruder moving picture sequence pointed up the obvious fact that, whatever each had reacted to, the reactions had occurred a second or so apart with the President reacting first. Probably, it was on the basis of this *seeming* discrepancy that *Life Magazine* titled the article: "Did Oswald act alone? A MATTER OF REASONABLE DOUBT."

It would seem that the great majority of Americans dutifully took all this in with varying degrees of interest and then very probably shrugged it off as a controversial issue beyond both arbitration and solution.

The author was about to do likewise, when, sometime during the last episode of the CBS Television broadcast, he suddenly became aware of what had occurred, ballistically, in the half-dozen seconds during which the President was shot to death and Governor Connally was seriously wounded.

The solution to what will hereinafter be referred to as *the mystery of the bullets* did not come to the author in a flash of mystic perception but seemed, rather, to have formed slowly as the criticisms and questions posed in the probings came into working agreement with the author's knowledge of high powered rifles and his long experience in investigating and reviewing climactic-type military incidents and accidents involving firearms.

What had actually happened in the half-dozen seconds during which the President had been assassinated became clear enough — three shots had been fired from a single location *and all three bullets had hit the President.*

At this point, it seemed reasonable to assume that such an occurrence had been equally clear to the Commission's investigators for them to have arrived at the basically correct conclusion that one assassin acting alone had killed the President and inadvertently wounded Governor Connally. Why, then, all the polemics, recriminations, and just plain

6

wrangling over the Warren Report? What justifications were there for all the wide-blown theories, probings, and criticisms?

The above questions sent the author packing off to the local book store for the paperback copy of the Warren Report, a copy of *The Witnesses*,[5] and copies of the half-dozen other publications that were on store shelves at the time criticizing or defending the President's Commission and its Report.

Anyone armed with the knowledge of what had happened to each of the three rifle bullets did not have to read very far into the early chapters of the Report to see that, although the Commission had arrived at a correct overall conclusion, its failure to determine the path and effect of each bullet and, more pointedly, its assumption that one of the bullets had missed even as large a target as the presidential limousine, had opened up a wide range of possibilities and by so doing had made President Kennedy and Governor Connally fair game for any critic or theorist who could conjure up a puff of smoke or the reverberation of a rifle shot.

It was plain enough to see that the Commission, as directed, had evaluated, rather than investigated, the circumstances surrounding the assassination of the President. The wording of the Report clearly demonstrated that the President's Commission had arrived at a correct overall conclusion by evaluative means, but, then, had made the serious investigative mistake of attempting to substantiate an evaluated conclusion by continuing on and trying to evaluate it in detail. The Commission and its staff and counsels, using evaluative procedures (and these poorly), had produced and recorded a narrative discussion of *what might have happened* during the shooting episode of the assassination.

This failure on the part of the Commission to give a definitive answer to the question of what had become of the three bullets fired at the presidential limousine clearly identified itself as the beginning point and underlying cause of the controversy that had developed over the findings of the Warren Report.

Nor was it necessary to read very far into the writings of the critics to ascertain that they too had uncovered the fact that the narrative discussions in Chapters II & III of the Report had done nothing more than ravel the shooting episode of the assassination into a mystery which, for all intents and purposes, invited all who read the Report to make their own determinations as to what might have come of the bullets fired at the presidential limousine.

It was clearly indicated in all these writings that the Commission's evaluations regarding the bullets did not provide (for the public mind) the finite determinations and proofs necessary to substantiate the Commission's principal conclusion that there had been only one assassin. Worse than that, their writings made it clear that the narrative discussion on what might have happened to the bullets not only failed to solve or prove anything, but mixed and muddled facts and suppositions into such a maze that they made no sense at all.

Only a brief perusal of the verbatim testimony contained in *The Witnesses* was necessary to see that, all unwittingly, the Commission's investigators had either overlooked, ignored, discredited or misinterpreted the testimony of the eyewitnesses riding in the presidential limousine, all of whom (including the President himself) furnish vital clues needed to solve the mystery of the bullets.

At this point in the author's research, it became apparent that the mystery of the bullets *was a mystery of the Commission's own making* and that the author, knowing its

8

solution, was uniquely situated to review and analyze the pertinent chapters of the Warren Report from the direction of enlightened retrospect.

This realization led to a more critical review of Chapters II & III of the Report which quickly identified the fundamental investigative mistakes and critical procedural errors committed by the Commission's investigators in their efforts to solve the mystery of the bullets. This, in turn, suggested the thought that the mystery could be solved using no more than the material evidence presented in the Warren Report, the eyewitness testimony of those persons riding with President Kennedy in the limousine, and the author's specialized training and experience.

The preceding thoughts became parents to the deed — a proper investigation was conducted which, as anticipated, led directly to and fully substantiated the author's out-of-hand determination of what had come of the bullets fired at the presidential limousine. Out of this investigation, once formally accomplished, came this book.

It is offered with the certain knowledge that it solves the mystery of the bullets — which solution, in turn, sets straight the controversial assassination sections of the Report.

But it does more than this. By fully substantiating (proving) the Commission's principal conclusion that a single assassin, acting alone, shot and killed President Kennedy and inadvertently wounded Governor Connally, it sets the entire record straight — and should, thereby, bring an end to a pointless controversy.

---

1 Bantam Book titled, *Report of the Warren Commission on the Assassination of President Kennedy.* Published in October, 1964, by Bantam Books, Inc.

2 Motion pictures taken on the scene of the assassination by an amateur photographer, Mr. Abraham Zapruder of Dallas, Texas. Film is now the property of *Life Magazine.*

3 Many references will be made to the individual Zapruder film frames which appear in the 25 November 1966 issue of *Life Magazine.*

4 Later to be called: The Single Bullet Theory.

5 Bantam Book titled: *The Witnesses,* published Dec., 1964.

Chapter II

THE TELLING OF IT

The chapters that follow contain two different stories covering the same brief period of time — the shooting episode (some 5.8 seconds) during which time President John F. Kennedy was assassinated and Governor John B. Connally, Jr., was severely wounded.

The stories have the same setting and both discourse at length on the subjects of bullets and rifle marksmanship. Each is trying to answer three basic, interconnected questions: "How many bullets were fired at the presidential limousine? From where were they fired? What was the order of firing, and path and effect of each bullet?"

The first story — PART II, THE STATUS QUO — is a critique on the Commission's estimate and evaluation of what occurred during the shooting episode of the assassination; and a critical look into the ramifications of its failure to give a substantive answer to the third question posed above.

11

The second story — PART III, WE (YOU & I) IN-VESTIGATE — is a programmed investigation of the mystery of the bullets — and its resolution.

There is little else in common between the two stories other than the basic theme and the ultimate conclusion of each that a single assassin shot and killed President Kennedy and wounded Governor Connally.

The continuity running through the entire narrative will be seen to parallel a mystery story — and a deep mystery it has become. As in detective fiction, there is a public clamor over the findings of the duly appointed investigators whose final report explains little else than how they got off the track in trying to solve what could well be called, The Case of the Missing Bullet — that Didn't Miss. Private investigators (you and I), with a different viewpoint, enter the case and, using the same evidence and testimony (and some specialized experience), readily solve the case.

The above parallel is by no means coincidental; it is a true reflection of existing circumstances.

The seven chapters that make up PARTS II and III are arranged and aligned to serve two distinct purposes.

The Investigative Purpose

It had been early noted that the critics of the Report usually premised their arguments against the Report on the assumption that the single assassin conclusion was in-correct in itself. Oddly enough, it was considered incorrect only because it was not properly substantiated in the official Report — which is illogical in itself.

It did follow, logically, that any theory involving additional assassins that the critics and theorists might project from such an illogical premise could very well prove to

12

be a wild-goose chase — if the single assassin conclusion was, in fact, correct.

As outlined in Chapter I, this reasoning led directly to the idea of taking the data, evidence and testimony contained in the Report and its supporting documentation and *investigating* rather than *evaluating* the single assassin conclusion to see if it could be properly substantiated. This led directly to a straight-line investigation of the mystery of the bullets — and to the formal solution documented herein.

There is nothing unusual or original in having decided to research the case from the angle that the single assassin conclusion was correct. The unusual thing, as the reader has been apprised, was the fortuitous dovetailing of personal experience with the probings of the critics and the press which caused the author to recognize the probable solution — long before he decided to enter into a formal investigation of the shooting episode of the assassination.

The following five chapters are aligned to recreate a comparable set of circumstances and, hopefully, a similar early enlightenment for the reader.

Accordingly:

He is read in on the key issues of the controversy that has grown up around the principal findings and conclusions of the published Report — Chapter III.

He is given an annotated look at the controversial sections of the Report that deal with the shooting episode of the assassination — Chapter IV.

He is briefed on the fundamental mistakes made by the Commission's investigators — Chapter V.

He is indoctrinated with the experienced investigator's attitude and outlook — Chapter VI.

He is given a suitable background of technical experience — Chapter VII.

Thus briefed and indoctrinated, he becomes a member of the investigating team and helps solve the mystery of the bullets — Chapter VIII.

. . . all of which places him in an informed position from which he can render reasoned judgments as to the validity — and the implications — of the major conclusions set forth in the official Report.

The Legal Purpose

When these two stories are put in literary sequence, with the Commission's inconclusive story first, a corollary finally emerges (following the solution presented in the second story) upon which a case can be made for the highly controversial supplementary conclusion of the Report that the single assassin was a specified person, namely — Lee Harvey Oswald.

Although a critic in this case, the author will be the Commission's advocate (heaven knows it needs one) and will act in support of its principal conclusion — but only insofar as it concluded that one assassin, acting alone, fired three rifle bullets at the President, thereby killing him. This includes support of the contingent conclusion that Governor Connally got caught in the single assassin's line of fire.

The author's brief in support of the single assassin conclusion of the official Report is as follows:

1. The single assassin conclusion contained in the Report is correct but, having been determined evaluatively, is not substantiated in legally sustainable determinations and proofs.

14

2. Lacking proper substantiation, this principal conclusion does not provide an adequate legal foundation upon which to indict the person proved in the Report to have been an assassin — as the sole assassin.

3. The solution of the mystery of the bullets, which the author has proved and formally documented in Chapter VIII herein, provides the necessary determinations and proofs to substantiate the conclusion set forth in the Report that there was only one assassin.

As the direct result of the foregoing:

The single assassin conclusion set forth by the President's Commission can be fully and properly substantiated with legally sustainable determinations and proofs.

Being so proved, the conclusion thereby provides an adequate legal basis upon which to indict the person proved in the Report to have been an assassin — as the sole assassin.

As attendant results:

The eyewitness accounts rendered by Governor and Mrs. John B. Connally, Jr., will be shown to have been true and correct in major detail.

The eyewitness accounts rendered by Mrs. John F. Kennedy and Secret Service Agent Roy H. Kellerman will be shown to have provided the final vital clues required to solve the mystery of the bullets.

The witch hunt for other assassins can finally be brought to a halt.

The author will feel that he has rendered a service to his country.

The reader is forewarned that he may encounter several twice-told tales and have to suffer through a certain amount of technical detail in the middle chapters of this book. This results, necessarily, from the requirements to brief the reader on critical technical factors, to set up the pattern and framework of an investigation, and to put together and execute the courtroom-like defense that is afforded the principal conclusion of the Warren Report.

But there are compensating factors. There is a continually building suspense and a piece by piece gathering and fitting together of technical data, material evidence, and logical deductions that will point up the solution of the central mystery long before the testimony of the final witness (Mrs. John F. Kennedy) is heard.

Finally, when the simple and uncomplicated solution is known, there will begin a growing amazement at how all the presently unexplained incidents and phenomena surrounding the shooting episode of the assassination suddenly become readily explainable — in the light of the correct solution.

Ultimately, it will be found that the application of the correct solution of the shooting episode even further substantiates and validates all other findings and conclusions set forth elsewhere in the body of the Report.

Part II

THE STATUS QUO

Chapter III

CRITICISMS

Why, indeed, has the Report become such a controversial document and why has the President's duly appointed Commission been lambasted from every direction? Why has this official report been challenged, discounted, and systematically discredited in the minutest detail?

Why have critics, with their new theories and innumerable interpretations, sprung up on every side to embarrass the Commission and disparage its Report?

The answers to these questions are exceedingly complex; in fact, they are unanswerable in any specific sense at this late date. One thing is plain enough, the underlying cause for such a totally adverse reaction is bound to lie in the official Report itself.

General

Any judgment as to how well the Commission performed its mission must be tempered with an understanding of what it was directed to do.

In broad terms, the Commission was appointed by the President (Lyndon Baines Johnson) and directed by him to ascertain, EVALUATE and report upon the facts relating to the assassination of the late President John F. Kennedy and the subsequent violent death of the man charged with the assassination.

In carrying out this encompassing directive, the President's Commission, necessarily, was required to gather and document a mass of essentially unrelated and often irrelevant material and information. In further execution of the letter of its directive, the Commission was called upon to evaluate this mass of data and, according to its judgements, to duly report its findings and conclusions to the President in the form of a narrative account — the so-called Warren Report.

The Report, after review by the United States Attorney General, was accepted by the President, thus becoming an Official Document of the United States Government.

That the President's Commission acted with the highest of motives and rendered its report in good faith and with a sincere desire to provide the Chief Executive with a comprehensive, conclusive and timely document — is beyond question. That it failed, in part, for lack of conclusiveness, is unfortunate. However, to distrust the entire report for this one reason is to overlook the important fact that the published Report has never yet had any of its principal findings or conclusions *proved* wrong.

If for no other reason than this, it behooves the American public, in its collective wisdom, to stand off and take a broader and more constructive look at this encompassing and extremely important public document.

Few realize that it was a discretionary move on the part

20

of the President that authorized the Report and its supporting files to become public documents. It is not to be denied that the President was under the considerable pressure of public interest, as incited by the more vehement critics, when he authorized the publication of the full Report and permitted access to its supporting documentation.

Considering the general reaction to the promulgation of the Report, it could be argued that the President made a strategic mistake when he authorized the publication (unabridged and unexpurgated) of a documentation representing the opinions of a selected group of men no longer officially commissioned to argue or defend either their reasoning processes or their stated judgments.

It could just as easily be argued that the President would have made a greater mistake if he had failed to exercise his discretionary powers in the face of the same strong pressure of public interest.

The Report Itself

As far as the Report itself is concerned, the author must find the Commission's investigators guilty of a serious error and a continuing neglect. Their serious error, as laboriously recorded in Chapter III of the Report, was their failure to solve the mystery of the bullets. Their continuing neglect was procedural — the rendering of a report, the nature of which almost insured against the solution ever coming to light — by any investigative means.

The author holds no personal brief for or against the Commission's investigators as regards their investigative ability or their capacity to reason correctly. It is appreciated that they functioned under a pressing directive to evaluate rather than to investigate, and certainly there is no question but that they did a prodigious job of searching

21

out information. The compilation and writing of the official Report itself was a task of monumental proportions.

Its evaluative approach baffles many people, very few of whom are familiar with the use and application of broad *evaluative reckonings* which finally become findings and conclusions in this very specialized type of report.

By its very proportions and composition, it is extremely vulnerable to destructive criticism and is bound to break down quickly under literal cross examination. It is easily misinterpreted and as easily misused — or abused — by those with ulterior motives or purposes.

It may be said that the Report not only opens itself up to criticism — its inconclusiveness invites it! The sections of the Report that deal with the shooting episode of the assassination so abound with unanswered (or poorly answered) questions, alternatives, and even riddles, that it is not difficult to understand why the critics, almost to a man, jumped squarely into its voids and vacuums and then, using the Report's own voluminous facts and figures, first tore it to ribbons and then wove some of the shreds back into their own theories or contentions.

The principal conclusion in the Report is that there was only one assassin who acted alone. It must be borne in mind that this is an *evaluated* judgement between one assassin — and more than one assassin, and that it was rendered only after a mountain of evidence and testimony had been reviewed and evaluated by the Commission.

There is no doubt but that it can be defended for what it is — an evaluated conclusion — and, as such, can be given certain investigative uses. Unfortunately, the Report used it legally — and mistakenly.

The first mistake made in the Report was to fail to discriminate between an assassin who participated in the assassination and a sole assassin. It went through a great

22

many words to identify an assassin and prove, beyond any doubt, that he had participated in the assassination. It then rendered an indictment against this *participating* assassin as the *sole* assassin on the legally (and investigatively) insufficient premise of its own *evaluated conclusion* that there had been only one assassin.

Technically, criminal indictment without legal sufficiency is an abridgment of the rights of an individual citizen of the United States. This, probably more than anything else, brought forth the barristers and the deeper thinking citizens to challenge the Report and its improper indictment of a dead man.

There is no question as to what brought forth the other great host of critics to do battle with the published Report. It was the Commission's failure to properly investigate, correctly determine, and properly report what actually occurred during the shooting episode of the assassination. In other words, its failure to solve the mystery of the bullets.

> Author's Comment: Just how the Commission's investigators, counsels, and commissioners managed to so thoroughly botch the job of investigating into the shooting episode of the assassination is a study in itself — and the subject of Chapter V of this book.

A Subtle Twist

The Commission made a peculiar blunder when, having arrived at its principal conclusion, it continued trying to further justify it — evaluatively. Its prolonged evaluative analysis of what might have happened, in Chapter III of the Report, not only invites criticisms and other solutions but, by a subtle twist of ideas, causes all who read and study it, to take up a track *away from the solution*.

23

It comes about in this fashion. With few exceptions, all who read or study the Report end up by disagreeing with the findings and conclusions that bear on the shooting episode of the assassination. This occurs because they quickly discern that the many evaluations and speculations set forth in Chapter III of the Report do not adequately support the conclusion that there was only one assassin. This disagreement with the evaluative technique used in this section of the Report has the effect of placing the reader in general opposition to the whole Report.

Here is the subtle twist to it. *The disagreement with the Commission's evaluations offered in support of its principal conclusion turns into a disagreement with the conclusion itself.*

To disagree with the conclusion that there was only one assassin is to contend that there was more than one assassin. This acquired belief that the single assassin conclusion is wrong then becomes the point of departure for wherever the search for *other assassins* may lead.

Not one of the published critics, it seems, has ever stopped criticizing long enough to consider the possibility that the single assassin conclusion might be correct — lacking only proper substantiation or proof. As this is the fact of the matter, it readily can be seen that most critics and theorists are on a futile quest because they are searching for things that do not exist — additional assassins.

Many interested citizens (critics in their own right) who take the trouble to read the sections of the Report dealing with the shooting episode of the assassination, also, are led astray. After tediously searching for bullets that missed, in Chapter III of the Report, they are bound to end up feeling that the Report put forth all the pertinent and material evidence necessary to prove its principal conclusion and then, for some undisclosed reason, failed

24

to form a connecting link between a good train of evidence and what might very well be a correct conclusion. Not having the training or experience necessary to rectify this apparent disjunction between good evidence and a correct conclusion, even these casual critics become victims of this subtle twist of ideas and they, too, depart in search of additional assassins — or the counsel of those critics or theorists who seem already to have found them.

Another large group of interested citizens who, also, have been diverted from the solution by reading the Report, somehow manage to sublimate this urge to strike out blindly in search of additional assassins. They apparently bring themselves to believe that the Commission may have inadvertently come upon the correct solution but that such a conclusion was either arbitrary, expedient, or at best, a compromise of many differing opinions within the Commission as to exactly what had occurred. These citizens, too, may end up under the spell of a publishing critic in their search for what they are sure exists — a clearer solution.

The Critics

Obviously, the writings of the critics have been more widely read than has the Report itself — the net result being that a great many more Americans know what is wrong with the Commission's Report than what is right with it.

Critics, pro and con, in championing their various views and theories, have extracted the Report extensively. Unfortunately for the Report, it has been extracted selectively and, more often than not, the extracts have been lifted (or bent) out of context. This practice, which has generated a number of seemingly plausible theories and solutions, has, on the other hand, seriously compromised

25

the Report by causing many readers (of criticisms) to exchange the basically correct findings and conclusions set forth in the Report for a regular hodgepodge of ill-conceived theories and ill-founded contentions.

As much as anything, it is this near encyclopedic outpouring of selected bits and pieces of the Report and its voluminous supporting documentation that has confused the reading public and saddled Americans generally (and a good part of the world) with a controversy that should not exist at all.

Some critics simply extract the Commission's own recorded data (tests, material evidence, testimony, evaluations, speculations, et al.), revamp its implications to suit themselves, and then use it to augment or shore up their own particular theories or contentions. Others seem to follow this same extracting and quoting routine, but for no other apparent purpose than to embarrass or discredit the President's Commission with its own words. Some, if the size and complexity of their publications and the originality and quality of their ideas are taken into literary (and investigative) account, can best be described as colossal nitpickers.

The published critics, like the casual critics, are no exception; they, too, are victims of this subtle twist to the Commission's evaluation of the shooting episode that causes people to disagree with its principal conclusion.

Certainly, their tactics vary considerably as they enter into battle with this formidable document called the Warren Report but, they too will all be seen to make the same mistake of immediately departing outward from the central fact of the matter to search for additional assassins or conspiracies.

26

There are those who attack the Report "tooth and nail" and all along the line, seemingly beset with an almost fanatical idea that the President's Commission was a conspiracy to begin with and, as such, functioned with deep conspiratorial motives and objectives. Each recorded error, inconsistency, inferential or evaluative comment, or just plain flub in this lengthy document becomes a purposeful deceit, a scheming plot, a conspiratorial design of near-international proportions.

These are the critics who go afield from where the Commission got off the track and create ever-deepening plots and conspiracies. Theirs is a world of deep intrigue, and they deal in ghostly men. If they do any harm, it is to the state of mind of those who read (and believe) their strange tales.

Then there are the detective critics who have entered into the controversy honestly believing that they can shed some light on Chapter III of the Report. They feel that they have good and sufficient evidence (and the investigative know-how) to solve the mystery of the bullets. Here again, we see the influence of this subtle twist in the Report. As they begin their investigations, we watch them depart steadily and surely on course — away from the solution. They invariably repeat all the mistakes made by the Commission's evaluators but, lacking an anchoring tie to the Commission's correctly evaluated principal conclusion, they are soon enmeshed in theories and solutions that border on the bizarre. Theirs is a pointless exercise that does little else than increase the size of the already large band of ghostly assassins who, it seems, must have been holding target practice in Dealey Plaza on that fateful day in November 1963.

Chapter IV

EXTRACTS FROM THE
OFFICIAL REPORT — Annotated

What follows are selected extracts from the text of the official Report. These particular sections have been selected, at the exclusion of others, because they bear directly on the shooting episode during which President Kennedy was killed and Governor Connally was seriously wounded.

They have not been extracted out of context but simply lifted out, verbatim, from their intermittant positions in the running narrative text of the Report.

Author's Note: The extracts appear in the same sequence as in the Report and are identified by their chapter and paragraph in the Report where possible.

Annotations will appear in the flow of the text as *(italicized)* words or phrases, e.g. *(incorrect)*, *(correct but wrong sequence)*, etc. Longer comments may

28

precede or follow the extract as *italicized* captions or postscripts.

The shooting episode of the Report is extracted and presented to the reader at this early point in the book for a number of reasons. The primary reason is, in truth, that there are no words with which to adequately describe this section of the Report — *its aberrant ramblings are a thing apart that must be seen to be believed.* However, the following specific reasons directly augment our investigative purpose.

1. To save the reader the task of researching the lengthy Report while giving him some familiarity with its rambling narrative style.

2. To present the Commission's story of the shooting episode of the assassination in the fullest possible form and context.

3. To let the reader see, first hand, the general vagueness and inconclusiveness of these sections of the Report.

4. To let the reader analyze for himself the many things that called out the critics to do battle with the Report.

5. To indicate, by annotation, the exact places in the narrative account where the Report is at variance with fact, true circumstance or actual happening — as known from *the correct solution.*

6. To provide a background against which to analyze and discuss the fundamental errors and missteps made by the Commission's investigators.

7. To show, first hand, the nature and extent of a dilemma from which the Commission could not extricate itself.

29

THE WARREN REPORT

— extracted —

CHAPTER I, SUMMARY AND CONCLUSIONS

Narrative of Events   (Bant-Rep p. 21)[1]

. . . . . .

The President's car which had been going north made a sharp turn toward the southwest onto Elm Street. At a speed of about 11 miles per hour, it started down the gradual descent toward a railroad overpass under which the motorcade would proceed before reaching the Stemmons Freeway. The front of the Texas School Book Depository was now on the President's right, and he waved to the crowd assembled there as he passed the building. Dealey Plaza — an open, landscaped area marking the western end of downtown Dallas — stretched out to the President's left. A Secret Service agent riding in the motorcade radioed the Trade Mart that the President would arrive in 5 minutes.

Seconds later shots resounded in rapid succession *(3 shots in 5.8 seconds)*. The President's hands moved to his neck *(moved, but not to his neck)*. He appeared to stiffen momentarily and lurch slightly forward in his seat. A bullet had entered the base of the back of his neck slightly to the right of the spine *(this wound not from first shot)*. It traveled downward and exited from the front of the neck, causing a nick in the lower portion of the knot in the President's necktie. Before the shooting started, Governor Connally had been facing toward the crowd on the right. He started to turn toward the left and suddenly

30

felt a blow on his back. The Governor had been hit by a bullet which entered at the extreme right side of his back at a point below his right arm pit. The bullet traveled through his chest in a downward and forward direction, exited below his right nipple, passed through his right wrist which had been in his lap, and then caused a wound to his left thigh *(all wounds from the second shot)*. The force of the bullet's impact appeared to spin the Governor to his right, and Mrs. Connally pulled him down into her lap. Another bullet *(from the third shot)* then struck President Kennedy in the rear portion of his head, causing a massive and fatal wound. The President fell to the left into Mrs. Kennedy's lap.

Secret Service Agent . . .

The conclusion At END OF Book is False!

. . . . . .

CONCLUSIONS (Bant-Rep pp. 37-39)

This Commission was created to ascertain the facts relating to the preceding summary of events and to consider the important questions which they raised. The Commission has addressed itself to this task and has reached certain conclusions based on all available evidence. No limitations have been placed on the Commission's inquiry; it has conducted its own investigation and all Government agencies have fully discharged their responsibility to cooperate with the Commission in its investigation. These conclusions represent the reasoned judgment *(but, unfortunately, diverse opinions)* of all members of the Commission and are presented after an investigation which has satisfied the Commission that it has ascertained the truth *(the truth, but not clarified or substantiated)* concerning the assassination of President Kennedy to the extent that

31

a prolonged and thorough *(but not conclusive)* search makes this possible.

1. The shots which killed President Kennedy and wounded Governor Connally were fired from the sixth-floor window at the southeast corner of the Texas School Book Depository *(correct)*. This determination is based upon the following:

(a) Witnesses at the scene of the assassination saw a rifle being fired from the sixth-floor window of the Depository Building, and some witnesses saw a rifle in the window immediately after the shots were fired *(all good corroborating evidence)*.

(b) The nearly whole bullet found on Governor Connally's stretcher at Parkland Memorial Hospital and the two bullet fragments found in the front seat of the presidential limousine were fired from the 6.5-millimeter Mannlicher-Carcano rifle found on the sixth floor of the Depository Building to the exclusion of all other weapons *(easily verified ballistically)*.

(c) The three used *(expended)* cartridge cases found near the window on the sixth floor at the southeast corner of the building were fired from the same rifle which fired the above-described bullet and fragments, to the exclusion of all other weapons *(easily verified ballistically)*.

(d) The windshield in the presidential limousine was struck by a bullet fragment on the inside surface of the glass but was not penetrated.

(e) The nature of the bullet wounds suffered by President Kennedy and Governor Connally and the location of the car *(presidential limousine)* at the time of the shots establish that the bullets were fired from above and behind the presidential limousine, striking the President and the Governor as follows:

(1) President Kennedy was first struck *(struck*

second time) by a bullet which entered at the back of his neck and exited through the lower front portion of his neck, causing a wound which would not necessarily have been fatal *(correct)*. The President was struck a second time *(third time)* by a bullet which entered the right rear portion of his head, causing a massive and fatal wound *(correct)*.

(2) Governor Connally was struck by a bullet which entered on the right side of his back and traveled downward through the right side of his chest, exiting below his right nipple. This bullet then passed through his right wrist and entered his left thigh where it caused a superficial wound *(all wounds from the second bullet fired)*.

(f) There is no credible evidence that the shots were fired from the Triple Underpass, ahead of the motorcade, or from any other location. *(No credible "material" evidence. A reasonable deduction if premised on the correct solution — an open invitation to critics, as the shooting sequence is described in the Warren Report.)*

2. The weight of the evidence indicates that there were three shots fired *(correct, necessarily an evaluated conclusion)*.

3. Although it is not necessary to any essential findings of the Commission to determine just which shot hit Governor Connally *(this happens to be the key to the solution)*, there is very persuasive evidence from the experts *(and everywhere else)* to indicate that the same bullet which pierced the President's throat also caused Governor Connally's wounds. *(It did in fact.)* However, Governor Connally's testimony *(which is a true and accurate account)* and certain other factors *(mainly the Single Bullet Theory)* have given rise to some difference of opinion *(should not have as they are entirely compatible)* as to this probability but there is no question in the mind of any member of

the Commission that all the shots which caused the President's and Governor Connally's wounds were fired from the sixth-floor window of the Texas School Book Depository.

> *The foregoing findings and conclusions are typical results of the evaluative process. They are seen to be an admixture of both factual and evaluated findings — seasoned with a liberal sprinkling of pure supposition. As such, they are useful only to those who deal in generalities or operate on very broad guidelines. They can be outright liabilities to those who must deal in specifics.*
>
> *If any particular thing can be said to have opened the wellspring from which so much adverse comment and criticism has come, it would be the Commission's failure to properly relate the order and sequence of major happenings during the shooting episode of the assassination with the sequence in which the shots were fired — and its failure to specifically determine the wound(s) inflicted by each bullet.*
>
> *The "declaration" in Paragraph 3 that it was not necessary to any essential findings of the Commission to determine just which shot hit Governor Connally is a classical example of what can happen when a fact is not truthfully stated to the American public. Better for the Commission to have confessed and stated that, "Although the Commission has not been able to determine (agree on) just which shot hit Governor Connally, it is not believed that such determination is necessary to any essential findings. . . ." Considering everything, especially the reaction that this rationalization of an investigative shortcoming called forth from the critics, this paragraph would have been better left unwritten.*

4. The shots which killed President Kennedy and wounded Governor Connally were fired by Lee Harvey Oswald. This conclusion is based on the following:

(a) The Mannlicher-Carcano . . .

. . . .

The foregoing paragraph specifically indicts Lee Harvey Oswald as the sole assassin. Following as it does on the heels of the combination of factual and evaluated findings and conclusions contained in Paragraphs 1, 2, and 3, above, it readily can be seen that this indictment is premised, in part, on evaluated evidence. Its legal insufficiency is apparent.

It is interesting to note that the factual evidence supporting Paragraph 4, above, (not extracted here), is legally sufficient to sustain an indictment of Lee Harvey Oswald as having fired the Mannlicher-Carcano rifle at the President during the assassination. In other words, it can be legally proved that Lee Harvey Oswald participated in the assassination.

CHAPTER II, THE ASSASSINATION

(Bant-Rep p. 47)

. . . . . .

Author's Comment: The following account of the shooting episode of the assassination is merely a repeat of the findings and conclusions contained in the preceding extracts — with a singular difference. In the following, the Commission has interjected the accounts (testimony) of key witnesses tailored, unwittingly, to fit the Commission's own inconclusive and basically incorrect conception of what had taken place during the shooting episode of the assassination.

All key witnesses give indications of having been led or prompted during their interrogations along the lines of the same misconceptions that, unfortunately, were misleading the Commission's own investigators. For example, it became common knowledge that the President had received a head wound and a throat wound. The Zapruder film sequence showed the head wound to be the last wound received by the President.

Therefore, reasoned the Commission, his appearing to react to a wound earlier in the film had to be *a reaction to the throat wound* — and all witnesses were interrogated accordingly.

Such questions as, "Did he appear to be grasping for his throat?" and "Were his hands at his throat like this . . . (demonstrating)?" solicited such answers as, "Something like that," or, "I suppose you could say he was." These then were taken by the Commission — as verifications.

The inadvertent leading of witnesses into verifying misconceptions is a common (and very disconcerting) investigative error — but one seldom made by an experienced investigator. The damage done to the Commission's "evaluations" is epitomized by the simple fact *that President Kennedy never did noticeably react to his throat wound.*

The following extracts have not been annotated; they are included here for reader interest and comparison purposes only.

· · · · · ·

The Assassination   (Bant-Rep p. 61)

At 12:30 P.M., CST as the President's open limousine proceeded at approximately 11 miles per hour along Elm Street toward the Triple Underpass, shots fired from a rifle mortally wounded President Kennedy and seriously injured Governor Connally. One bullet passed through the President's neck; a subsequent bullet, which was lethal, shattered the right side of his skull. Governor Connally sustained bullet wounds in his back, the right side of his chest, right wrist and left thigh.

· · · · · ·

The Speed of the Limousine   (Bant-Rep p. 62)

William Greer, operator of the presidential limousine, estimated the car's speed at the time of the first shot as 12 to 15 miles per hour. Other witnesses in the motorcade estimated the speed of the President's limousine from 7 to 22 miles per hour. A more precise determination has been made from motion pictures taken on the scene by an amateur photographer, Abraham Zapruder. Based on these films, the speed of the President's automobile is computed at an average speed of 11.2 miles per hour. The car maintained this average over a distance of approximately 136 feet immediately preceding the shot which struck the President in the head. While the car traveled this distance, the Zapruder camera ran 152 frames. Since the camera operates at a speed of 18.3 frames per second, it was calculated that the car required 8.3 seconds to cover the 136 feet. This represents a speed of 11.2 miles per hour.

In the Presidential Limousine (Bant-Rep pp. 62-63)

Mrs. John F. Kennedy, on the left of the rear seat of the limousine, looked toward her left and waved to the crowds along the route. Soon after the motorcade turned onto Elm Street, she heard a sound similar to a motorcycle noise and a cry from Governor Connally, which caused her to look to her right. On turning she saw a quizzical look on her husband's face as he raised his left hand to his throat. Mrs. Kennedy then heard a second shot and saw the President's skull torn open under the impact of the bullet. As she cradled her mortally wounded husband, Mrs. Kennedy cried, "Oh, my God, they have shot my husband, I love you, Jack."

Governor Connally testified that he recognized the first

37

noise as a rifle shot and the thought immediately crossed his mind that it was an assassination attempt. From his position on the right jump seat immediately in front of the President, he instinctively turned to his right because the shot appeared to come from over his right shoulder. Unable to see the President as he turned to the right, the Governor started to look back over his left shoulder, but he never completed the turn because he felt something strike him in the back. In his testimony before the Commission, Governor Connally was certain that he was hit by the second shot, which he stated he did not hear.

Mrs. Connally, too, heard a frightening noise from her right. Looking over her right shoulder, she saw that the President had both hands at his neck but she observed no blood and heard nothing. She watched as he slumped down with an empty expression on his face. Roy Kellerman, in the right front seat of the limousine, heard a report like a firecracker pop. Turning to his right in the direction of the noise, Kellerman heard the President say, "My God, I am hit," and saw both of the President's hands move up toward his neck. As he told the driver, "Let's get out of here; we are hit," Kellerman grabbed his microphone and radioed ahead to the lead car, "We are hit. Get us to the hospital immediately."

The driver, William Greer, heard a noise which he took to be a backfire from one of the motocycles flanking the presidential car. When he heard the same noise again, Greer glanced over his shoulder and saw Governor Connally fall. At the sound of the second shot he realized that something was wrong and he pressed down on the accelerator as Kellerman said, "Get out of here fast." As he issued his instructions to Greer and to the lead car, Kellerman heard a "flurry of shots" within 5 seconds of the first noise. According to Kellerman, Mrs. Kennedy then cried out:

"What are they doing to you?" Looking back from the front seat, Kellerman saw Governor Connally in his wife's lap and Special Agent Clinton J. Hill lying across the trunk of the car.

Mrs. Connally heard a second shot fired and pulled her husband down into her lap. Observing his blood-covered chest as he was pulled into his wife's lap, Governor Connally believed himself mortally wounded. He cried out, "Oh, no, no, no. My God, they are going to kill us all." At first Mrs. Connally thought that her husband had been killed, but then she noticed an almost imperceptible movement and knew that he was still alive. She said, "It's all right. Be still." The Governor was lying with his head on his wife's lap when he heard a shot hit the President. At that point, both Governor and Mrs. Connally observed brain tissue splattered over the interior of the car. According to Governor and Mrs. Connally, it was after this shot that Kellerman issued his emergency instruction and the car accelerated.

Reaction by the Secret Service Agents

(Bant-Rep pp. 63-64)

From the left front running board of the President's followup car, Special Agent Hill was scanning the few people standing on the south side of Elm Street after the motorcade had turned off Houston Street. He estimated that the motorcade had slowed down to approximately 9 or 10 miles per hour on the turn at the intersection of Houston and Elm Streets and then proceeded at a rate of 12 to 15 miles per hour with the followup car trailing the President's automobile by approximately 5 feet. Hill heard a noise, which seemed to be a firecracker, coming from his right rear. He immediately looked to his right, "and, in so doing, my eyes had to cross the presidential limousine and I saw President Kennedy grab at himself and lurch forward and to the left." Hill jumped from the followup car and ran to the President's. . . .

. . . . .

CHAPTER III. THE SHOTS FROM THE TEXAS BOOK DEPOSITORY – annotated –

. . . . .

The Shot that Missed   (Bant-Rep p. 107)

From the initial finding that (a) one shot passed through the President's neck and then most probably passed through the Governor's body *(true enough)*, (b) a subsequent shot penetrated the President's head *(true enough)*, (c) no other shot struck any other part of the automobile *(so proved)*, and (d) three shots were fired *(a reasonable deduction)*, it follows that one probably missed the car *(this follows)* and its occupants *(this does not follow)*. The evidence is inconclusive as to whether it was the first, second, or third shot which missed.

> Author's Comment: The foregoing narrative conclusion will be elaborated on because it is probably the best example of the illogical twist that the Commission applied to all its findings and conclusions regarding the three shots and their sequential effects.
>
> Such an "it follows" conclusion (syllogistical deduction) as that above is correct only when all premises are correct — and inclusive. The premise that is entirely lacking in the above to validate the conclusion is a statement to the effect that "no occupant was

struck by a bullet otherwise than as evidenced by wounds." It would then follow, logically, that one shot missed the car "and its occupants."

But the Commission could make no such statement, nor could it have proved such a statement if made — because an occupant was struck otherwise than as evidenced by a wound. But we are getting ahead of our story.

The fact remains that the President was struck otherwise — *which is another way of saying that no bullet missed!* If no bullet missed, the Commission's statement that, "The evidence is inconclusive as to whether it was the first, second, or third shot which missed," becomes apropos of nothing, and the long evaluative analyses that follow this statement in the Report as to which of the three bullets "may have missed" becomes one step farther removed from apropos of nothing.

However, they are presented here in full context for a purpose. When the reader has gained the solution (in Chapter VIII), he is invited to turn back and read these analyses of the bullet that may have missed. He will be surprised to find that there is a great deal of sound argument and evidence presented in these three analyses which is strong corroborative evidence for the correct solution.

It might prove interesting for the reader to scan through them now just to see how far afield the (uncontrolled) evaluative process can take an investigator — once he gets off the track.

They have not been annotated for obvious reasons — the reader will be fully capable of doing it himself, when he returns with the correct solution.

The First Shot   (Bant-Rep pp. 108-109)

If the first shot missed, the assassin perhaps missed in an effort to fire a hurried shot before the President passed under the oak tree, or possibly he fired as the President passed under the tree and the tree obstructed his view. The

41

bullet might have struck a portion of the tree and been completely deflected. On the other hand, the greatest cause for doubt that the first shot missed is the improbability that the same marksman who twice hit a moving target would be so inaccurate on the first and closest of his shots as to miss completely, not only the target, but the large automobile.

Some support for the contention that the first shot missed is found in the statement of Secret Service Agent Glen A. Bennett, stationed in the right rear seat of the President's followup car, who heard a sound like a firecracker as the motorcade proceeded down Elm Street. At that moment, Agent Bennett stated:

. . . I looked at the back of the President. I heard another firecracker noise and saw that shot hit the President about four inches down from the right shoulder. A second shot followed immediately and hit the right rear high of the President's head. . . .

Substantial weight may be given Bennett's observations. Although his formal statement was dated November 23, 1963, his notes indicate that he recorded what he saw and heard at 5:30 P.M., November 22, 1963, on the airplane enroute back to Washington, prior to the autopsy, when it was not yet known that the President had been hit in the back. It is possible, of course, that Bennett did not observe the hole in the President's back, which might have been there immediately after the first noise.

Governor Connally's testimony supports the view that the first shot missed, because he stated that he heard a shot, turned slightly to his right, and, as he started to turn back toward his left, was struck by the second bullet. He never saw the President during the shooting sequence, and it is entirely possible that he heard the missed shot and that both men were struck by the second bullet. Mrs. Connally testified that after the first shot she turned and saw the President's hands moving toward his throat, as seen

42

in the films at frame 225. However, Mrs. Connally further stated that she thought her husband was hit immediately thereafter by the second bullet. If the same bullet struck both the President and the Governor, it is entirely possible that she saw the President's movements at the same time as she heard the second shot. Her testimony, therefore, does not preclude the possibility of the first shot having missed.

Other eyewitness testimony, however, supports the conclusion that the first of the shots fired hit the President. As discussed in Chapter II, Special Agent Hill's testimony indicates that the President was hit by the first shot and that the head injury was caused by a second shot which followed about 5 seconds later. James W. Altgens, a photographer in Dallas for the Associated Press, had stationed himself on Elm Street opposite the Depository to take pictures of the passing motorcade. Altgens took a widely circulated photograph which showed President Kennedy reacting to the first of the two shots which hit him. (See Commission Exhibit No. 900.) According to Altgens, he snapped the picture "almost simultaneously" with a shot which he is confident was the first one fired. Comparison of his photograph with the Zapruder film, however, revealed that Altgens took his picture at approximately the same moment as frame 255 of the movie, 30 to 45 frames (approximately 2 seconds) later than the point at which the President was shot in the neck. (See Commission Exhibit No. 901.) Another photographer, Phillip L. Willis, snapped a picture at a time which he also asserts was simultaneous with the first shot. Analysis of his photograph revealed that it was taken at approximately frame 210 of the Zapruder film, which was the approximate time of the shot that probably hit the President and the Governor. If Willis accurately recalled that there were no previous shots, this would be strong evidence that the first shot did not miss.

If the first shot did not miss, there must be an explanation for Governor Connally's recollection that he was not hit by it. There was, conceivably, a delayed reaction between the time the bullet struck him and the time he realized that he was hit, despite the fact that the bullet struck a glancing blow to a rib and penetrated his wrist bone. The Governor did not even know that he had been struck in the wrist or in the thigh until he regained consciousness in the hospital the next day. Moreover, he testified that he did not hear what he thought was the second shot, although he did hear a subsequent shot which coincided with the shattering of the President's head. One possibility, therefore, would be a sequence in which the Governor heard the first shot, did not immediately feel the penetration of the bullet, then felt the delayed reaction of the impact on his back, later heard the shot which shattered the President's head, and then lost consciousness without hearing a third shot which might have occurred later.

The Second Shot (Bant-Rep pp. 109-110)

The possibility that the second shot missed is consistent with the elapsed time between the two shots that hit their mark. From the timing evidenced by the Zapruder films, there was an interval of from 4.8 to 5.6 seconds between the shot which struck President Kennedy's neck (between frames 210 and 225) and the shot which struck his head at frame 313. Since a minimum of 2.3 seconds must elapse between shots, a bullet could have been fired from the rifle and missed during this interval. This possibility was buttressed by the testimony of witnesses who claimed that the shots were evenly spaced, since a second shot occurring

44

within an interval of approximately 5 seconds would have to be almost exactly midway in this period. If Altgens' recollection is correct that he snapped his picture at the same moment as he heard a shot, then it is possible that he heard a second shot which missed, since a shot fired 2.3 seconds before he took his picture at frame 255 could have hit the President at about frame 213.

On the other hand, a substantial majority of the witnesses stated that the shots were not evenly spaced. Most witnesses recalled that the second and third shots were bunched together, although some believed that it was the first and second which were bunched. To the extent that reliance can be placed on recollection of witnesses as to the spacing of the shots, the testimony that the shots were not evenly spaced would militate against a second shot missing. Another factor arguing against the second shot missing is that the gunman would have been shooting at very near the minimum allowable time to have fired the three shots within 4.8 to 5.6 seconds, although it was entirely possible for him to have done so. (See Ch. IV.)

The Third Shot (Bant-Rep pp. 110-112)

The last possibility, of course, is that it was the third shot which missed. This conclusion conforms most easily with the probability that the assassin would most likely have missed the farthest shot, particularly since there was an acceleration of the automobile after the shot which struck the President's head. The limousine also changed direction by following the curve to the right, whereas previously it had been proceeding in almost a straight line with a rifle protruding from the sixth-floor window of the Depository Building.

One must consider, however, the testimony of the witnesses who described the head shot as the concluding event in the assassination sequence. Illustrative is the testimony of the Associated Press photographer Altgens, who had an excellent vantage point near the President's car. He recalled that the shot which hit the President's head "was the last shot — that much I will say with a great degree of certainty." On the other hand, Emmett J. Hudson, the groundskeeper of Dealey Plaza, testified that from his position on Elm Street, midway between Houston Street and the Triple Underpass, he heard a third shot after the shot which hit the President in the head. In addition, Mrs. Kennedy's testimony indicated that neither the first nor the second shot missed. Immediately after the first noise, she turned, because of the Governor's yell, and saw her husband raise his hand to his forehead. Then the second shot struck the President's head.

Some evidence suggested that the third shot may have entirely missed and hit the turf or street by the Triple Underpass. Royce G. Skelton, who watched the motorcade from the railroad bridge, testified that after two shots "the car came on down close to the Triple Underpass" and an additional shot "hit in the left front of the President's car on the cement." Skelton thought that there had been a total of four shots, either the third or fourth of which hit in the vicinity of the underpass. Dallas Patrolman J. W. Foster, who was also on the Triple Underpass, testified that a shot hit the turf near a manhole cover in the vicinity of the underpass. Examination of this area, however, disclosed no indication that a bullet struck at the locations indicated by Skelton or Foster.

At different locations in Dealey Plaza, the evidence indicated that a bullet fragment did hit the street. James T. Tague, who got out of his car to watch the motorcade from a position between Commerce and Main streets near the Triple Underpass, was hit on the cheek by an object during the shooting. Within a few minutes Tague reported this to Deputy Sheriff Eddy R. Walthers, who was examining the area to see if any bullets had struck the turf. Walthers immediately started to search where Tague had been standing and located a place on the south curb of Main Street where it appeared a bullet had hit the cement. According to Tague, "There was a mark quite obviously that was a bullet, and it was very fresh." In Tague's opinion, it was the second shot which caused the mark, since he thinks he heard the third shot after he was hit in the face. This incident appears to have been recorded in the contemporaneous report of Dallas Patrolman L. L. Hill, who radioed in around 12:40 P.M.: "I have one guy that was possibly hit by a ricochet from the bullet off the concrete." Scientific examination of the mark on the south curb of Main Street by FBI experts disclosed metal smears which "were spectrographically determined to be essentially lead with a trace of antimony." The mark on the curb could have originated from the lead core of a bullet but the absence of copper precluded "the possibility that the mark on the curbing section was made by an unmutilated military full metal-jacketed bullet such as the bullet from Governor Connally's stretcher."

It is true that the noise of a subsequent shot might have been drowned out by the siren on the Secret Service followup car immediately after the head shot, or the dramatic effect of the head shot might have caused so much confusion that the memory of subsequent events was blurred. Nevertheless, the preponderance of the eyewitness testimony that the head shot was the final shot must be weighed in any determination as to whether it was the third shot that missed. Even if it were caused by a bullet fragment, the mark on the south curb of Main Street cannot be identified conclusively with any of the three shots fired. Under the circumstances it might have come from the bullet which hit the President's head, or it might have been a product of the fragmentation of the missed shot hitting some other object in the area. Since he did not observe any of the shots striking the President, Tague's testimony that the second shot, rather than the third, caused the scratch on his cheek, does not assist in limiting the possibilities.

The wide range of possibilities and the existence of conflicting testimony, when coupled with the impossibility of scientific verification, precludes a conclusive finding by the Commission as to which shot missed.

TIME SPAN OF SHOTS   (Bant-Rep p. 112)

Here again, the Commission's evaluations are premised on misconceptions of bullet sequence and effect, and so, are of little value to the trained investigator other than to furnish the broad working conclusion that the shots were fired after the presidential limousine had turned onto Elm Street and before it passed into the Triple Underpass.

Witnesses at the assassination scene said that the shots were fired within a few seconds, with the general estimate being 5 to 6 seconds. That approximation was most probably based on the earlier publicized reports that the first shot struck the President in the neck, the second wounded the Governor and the third shattered the President's head, with the time span from the neck to the head shots on the President being approximately 5 seconds. As previously indicated, the time span between the shot entering the back of the President's neck and the bullet which shattered his skull was 4.8 to 5.6 seconds. If the second shot missed, then 4.8 to 5.6 seconds was the total time span of the shots. If either the first or third shots missed, then a minimum of 2.3

48

seconds (necessary to operate the rifle) must be added to the time span of the shots which hit, giving a minimum time of 7.1 to 7.9 seconds for the three shots. If more than 2.3 seconds elapsed between a shot that missed and one that hit, then the time span would be correspondingly increased.

CONCLUSION (Bant-Rep p. 112)

Based on the evidence analyzed in this chapter, the Commission has concluded that the shots which killed President Kennedy and wounded Governor Connally were fired from the sixth-floor window at the southeast corner of the Texas School Book Depository Building. Two bullets probably caused all the wounds suffered by President Kennedy and Governor Connally. Since the preponderance of the evidence indicated that three shots were fired, the Commission concluded that one shot probably missed the presidential limousine and its occupants, and that the three shots were fired in a time period ranging from approximately 4.8 to in excess of 7 seconds.

(Thus ends Chapter III of the Warren Report)

---

1 This "reader's reference" has been inserted throughout this chapter to aid those who desire to read the full context out of which the extract has been drawn. General reference (previously cited) is to Bantam Book titled, "Report of the Warren Commission on the Assassination of President Kennedy," published October, 1964. Specific reference, (Bant-Rep pp. _____), designates the pages in this Bantam Book publication wherein this particular extract from the Report can be found.

Chapter V

OFF THE TRACK

In the beginning, the President's Commission made the evaluation correctly enough that three shots had been fired in the direction of the presidential limousine from a rifleman's post on the sixth floor of the Texas School Book Depository.

With three shots and three wounds to go on, it looked like an open-and-shut case to everyone. With the aid of the Abraham Zapruder moving picture sequence, it appeared clear enough that the first shot had hit the President in the neck, the second had hit Governor Connally in the back, and the third shot had hit the President again causing a massive head wound. Most eyewitness accounts, and the wounds themselves, indicated that all three shots had come from a position behind the line of travel of the presidential limousine down Elm Street.

It was not only an open-and-shut case as far as the

shooting was concerned, it was also a good case for only one assassin.

After a high powered rifle and three expended cartridge cases were found near the suspected assassin's post, it became an open-and-shut case — against a single assassin.

What, then, went wrong?

Ironically, what went wrong was the only sound piece of investigative deduction accomplished by the Commission during its investigation of the shooting episode of the assassination.

A member of the Commission's investigating staff, Attorney Arlen Specter, after studying the wound reports, deduced (and correctly) that the bullet which had pierced the President's neck, had passed clean through his neck, and had continued on, almost unimpeded, in a downward direction towards Governor Connally's position in the presidential limousine.

This probability (which bordered on certainty) that the passage of a single bullet had caused the President's neck wound and Governor Connally's multiple wounds — the so-called Single Bullet Theory — can, in retrospect, be identified as the catalytic agent that caused the Commission's investigators to make their first serious mistakes which, in turn, insured right at the start that they would never solve the mystery of the bullets.

The Fundamental Mistakes

With the correct solution at hand, it is not difficult to determine just where the Commission's investigators got off the track in trying to solve the mystery of the bullets. Probably it would better be said that they never got on the track of the solution in the first place.

Their having started out with what appeared to be an

open-and-shut case against the lone rifleman in the sixth-floor window of the Depository, fixed two preconceptions in the minds of the Commission's investigators which they would not relinquish even when the Single Bullet Theory emerged and forced them to take a more careful look at the shooting episode of the assassination.

The first of these preconceptions was that the President's neck wound was the first injury suffered by the President. The second, growing out of the first, was that the President was reacting to this neck wound when he came back into camera view from behind the road sign in frame No. 225 in the Zapruder film sequence.[1]

The emergence of the Single Bullet Theory and the adoption of the two preconceptions noted above undoubtedly set the stage for, and prompted, the type of reasoning that led the Commission's investigators away from the solution to the mystery of the bullets and deeper and deeper into a self-generated dilemma.

It was early in the investigation that the Commission made its first serious investigative misstep — it incorporated the two preconceptions (both erroneous) into its evaluation of the single bullet concept.

Because of these erroneous preconceptions, the President's neck wound, as mistakenly read into Zapruder film frame No. 225, appeared to have been inflicted the better part of a second before Governor Connally appeared (in the film) to have received his wounds. This failure of the two men to react simultaneously to the single bullet became one of several strong arguments (within the Commission) against the probability of one bullet having struck both men.

The relegation of the single bullet concept to the status of a mere "theory" by the greater part of the Commission made it almost certain that this unbelieving group would never solve the mystery of the bullets. The believers

52

in the single bullet concept, the minority, were led by the erroneous preconceptions into making an equally serious investigative blunder. The *seeming* fact that the two men had not reacted simultaneously to the impact of the single bullet caused them to discount, if not actually doubt, the exceedingly important (and correct) eyewitness accounts of Governor and Mrs. Connally which, even when repeated today, emphasize that Governor Connally was hit by the second shot and at the point where he appears to begin to react to having been struck at about Zapruder film frame No. 236.

This split opinion within the Commission on the single bullet concept undoubtedly led to a variety of opinions on the value and use of this vital testimony and the testimony of other eyewitnesses riding in the presidential limousine and in the followup vehicle.

All the foregoing was bad enough and, by itself, would have insured that the President's Commission, as a group, would never see even a glimmer of the solution to the mystery of the bullets. But misconception, like preconception, is a highly communicable disease among investigators and, in the Commission's case, it spread rapidly among its interrogators and counsels, if not among the Commissioners themselves. This became most evident in the interrogations — hardly a witness was spared a line of questioning that was not predicated on an erroneous preconception or tied in with a misconception.

As with erroneous preconceptions, it is equally damaging to the deductive reasoning process to allow early assumptions to become rigid and controlling criteria. The Commission committed this serious investigative error when it took the results of several empirical firing tests performed by other Governmental agencies and, from them,

53

summarily established the rigid criterion that the bolt-action Mannlicher-Carcano military rifle could not be operated (reloaded) and fired at a rate faster than a shot every 2.3 seconds — and still attain the accuracy allegedly demonstrated by the assassin shooting from the sixth-floor window of the Depository.

A good many of the procedural errors and investigative missteps made by the Commission grew out of its very organizational structure. It was directed to evaluate data gathered more or less at random and it was organized to do just that. Staff-wise, it was divided into interrogation teams which supplied data to evaluating teams. As the Commission's search was in the direction of any and all related circumstances, the data thus gathered must have been evaluated independently within major search areas. Technical and test data was supplied from other Governmental agencies. In short, the President's Commission was organized to *evaluate* the circumstances surrounding the assassination of a President of the United States of America — it was not organized to *investigate into* just a shooting incident.

The best way to explain the foregoing statements is to briefly describe the operation of a group specifically organized to investigate into shooting incidents — without particular regard for the rank or eminence (no disrespect intended) of the victims.

True investigating groups work in an entirely different pattern than do evaluating groups. First, the SCOPE of the investigation is determined. This amounts to identifying and delimiting exactly what is to be investigated. Once the scope of the investigation is determined and definitive limits are set, INVESTIGATIVE CONTROL must be established.

This can be the most difficult part of setting up an investigation. It amounts to identifying certain points of reference — factual guideposts, so to speak — along the center line or main track of the circumstance under investigation. Once these factual guideposts or tie-in points are established, all evidence, testimony, and time sequencing, must be checked against them. Nothing is interjected into the deductive reasoning process until proven relevant, material, consistent, and to have bearing on the segment of the circumstance under investigation. It is a controlled technical process that allows little room for general theories or broad evaluations.

As previously discussed, the President's Commission arrived at the conclusion that there was only one assassin as the net result of evaluating all factors related to the assassination. Witness another of its recorded conclusions: "There is no credible evidence that the shots were fired from the Triple Underpass, ahead of the motorcade, or from any other location." In other words, the shots could have come only from the sixth-floor window of the Texas School Book Depository because no credible evidence, in the great mass of evidence gathered, showed that bullets had come from anywhere else. This broad evaluation carries with it, inferentially, the conclusion that there was only one bolt-action rifle firing at the presidential limousine and, therefore, there could have been only one assassin firing at the President. There is no question but that these, within themselves, are entirely reasonable evaluative conclusions.

When it was called upon to investigate down into the immediate details and specifics of the shooting episode of the assassination, the President's Commission continued to do what it had been directed to do — to evaluate! So, it was preordained that the Commission would violate every rule of good investigative procedure that there is in the book.

The unfortunate result of this near-comedy of investigative errors was, by the Commission's own admittance in its Report, its failure to definitively resolve the mystery of the bullets. Under the circumstances, it did the next best thing that evaluators can do — it evaluated and laboriously recorded all the things that made the shooting episode of the assassination "a puzzlement" to them.

Having arrived at its principal conclusion otherwise than through definitive investigative procedures, it is not likely that the Commission felt any pressing requirement, considering its broad directive, to solve the mystery of the bullets in legal detail.

The Resultant Dilemma

By definition, a dilemma is an argument presenting an antagonist with two or more alternatives (or "horns") which are equally conclusive against him, whichever he chooses.

It is plain to see that the Commission's investigators did exactly this to themselves in trying to solve the mystery of the bullets — and duly recorded their predicament in the official Report.

As previously noted, the emergence of the single bullet concept kept the original open-and-shut case that had been so easily evaluated — from shutting.

If the Commission adopted the single bullet concept, it then had a problem with the three bullets which, according to its previous determinations, had been fired at the presidential limousine. If one bullet caused both of them to be wounded and another bullet caused only one wound (the President's final head wound), which accounts for all the major wounds found, *then one of the three bullets fired did not cause a wound.* If it did not cause a wound, what did it do? This is the question that the adoption of the single bullet concept posed to the Commission's investigators — a question that they were not even able to agree on, let alone answer satisfactorily.

In any event, the Commission now had a missing bullet; in fact, it had a bullet that apparently had just disappeared into thin air without leaving a trace. This "shot that missed," as the Commission qualifies it in the official Report, became the first "horn" of its developing dilemma.

If the Commission did not adopt the single bullet concept, then it was back to the open-and-shut solution — that the first bullet had hit the President in the neck, the second had struck Governor Connally in the back, and the third had hit the President in the back of his head and caused the massive head wound actually witnessed by many of the onlookers. But now, in the face of the evidence that had generated the single bullet concept, the Commission had to give a better accounting of the first bullet which, according to the Commission, *had hit the President in the neck.*

Credible evidence and autopsy data indicated that a bullet had passed clean through the President's neck which meant that it could only have continued on its course — straight for Governor Connally's back. But it could not have hit Governor Connally because, according to this line of deduction, he was hit later by the second bullet. So, if it did not hit Governor Connally, it must have buried itself in the presidential limousine — but it did not. The only possible answer left to the Commission was that the first bullet had disappeared into thin air somewhere be-

57

tween the President's neck and Governor Connally's back —
which posed the second "horn" of its dilemma.

A third "horn" appeared when the Commission tried to
fit the apparent reactions (to having been struck) of the
President and Governor Connally to the impact effects of
the single bullet that, according to the single bullet concept, would have struck both men simultaneously. Here
again, of course, things did not fit. The Zapruder film
sequence clearly showed the President reacting at least
one second before Governor Connally reacted.

A rationalization put forth by advocates of the single
bullet concept was that Governor Connally, although
struck simultaneously with the President, had had a delayed
reaction. This "out" was countered by Governor Connally
himself who emphatically maintained that he was hit at
the point where the Zapruder film shows him to have been
hit (frames 234-236), and that he had heard a rifle shot
before he felt the *single bullet* strike him.

This particular "horn" turned out to have two prongs.
Not only was the reaction of the two men out of phase a
second or so but the bullet's path through the President's
body, as shown by autopsy findings and clothing punctures,
was out of alignment with the trajectory of a bullet shown
to have been fired downward from the elevated sixth-floor
window of the Depository.

The Commission's erroneous preconception that the
first wound received by the President was his neck wound,
entailed a further conclusion that he had received it while
he was sitting bolt upright, with head erect, and while
waving an elevated right arm to the people on his right.
By all logic, the path of the bullet through his body (neck)
should have been downward.

Unfortunately for the Commission, when the bullet's

path through the President's back and neck is oriented relative to the President's body in a bolt-upright position — *it appears to pass through him on the level or on a slightly upward course* going from the point of entry in his back to the point of exit at the necktie-knot level of his throat.

Critics, generally, were quick to note and capitalize on this discrepancy — *which, in fact, exists.* So, the dilemma deepens and the criticisms intensify.

As seen in "Extracts from the Official Report — Annotated" (Chapter IV), the President's Commission found no way out of its dilemma, so, it found no solution to the mystery of the bullets. It ended up, in its Report, offering only the broad evaluative probabilities *that one bullet must have missed everything,* one might have wounded both men, and a third obviously struck the President in the back of the head — and killed him.

Such an answer, of course, brought up a bristle of "horns" for the Commission's investigators — which, in turn, left a host of unanswered questions for the lurking critics. If one bullet missed everything, how could it have missed everything? If one missed everything, which of the three was it? How, under the circumstances, could a bullet possibly miss everything? And so on, and so on.

The valiant, though futile, efforts put forth by the Commission in trying to answer these questions in an attempt to extricate itself from its self-imposed dilemma fill many pages of the official Report. It is entirely possible, considering the many other circumstances covered in the Report, that those on the Commission who assembled the Report never fully appreciated the extent of the dilemma that they had inflicted upon themselves or how completely their lengthy (evaluative) writings concealed the

correct solution to a mystery that was as self-generated —
as their dilemma was self-imposed.

One thing can be said for sure: the sections of the
Report that try to explain the shooting episode of the
assassination have provided most of the grist that the
critics have been grinding.

---

1 The individual picture frames of the Zapruder moving picture film
were numbered consecutively starting with No. 1, which began as the
presidential limousine turned onto Elm Street from Houston Street and
continued until the limousine disappeared into the Triple Underpass.
It is a continuous sequence through the shooting episode of the assassination.

Part III

WE (YOU AND I) INVESTIGATE

Chapter VI

A CHANGE OF VIEWPOINT

We have come to the end of the first story and now stand at the beginning of the second.

Briefly reviewing Part II, we note that the reader has been looking at the circumstances related to the assassination of President John F. Kennedy from the Commission's (and the critics) direction of view — with the word direction used advisedly. We have been brought to realize that the President's Commission, by its very directive, was required to look from the outside in. It had to be looking inwardly and evaluatively from the vast perimeter of gathered facts and fictions relating to both the President's death and the death of the man charged with his assassination.

Unquestionably, it was this broad evaluative approach that led the Commission's investigators to the reasonable (and correct) conclusion that, considering all probabilities, there had been only one assassin who acted alone.

We have seen that the perseverance of the Commission's investigators in continuing to *evaluate* rather than *investigate* the specific acts of violence that killed the President entangled them in a web of possibilities which finally became a dilemma from which they could not extricate themselves.

Certainly, we have come to appreciate that the Commission was under Presidential directive to *collect and evaluate* all related facts and circumstances and that it did this job admirably well.

In the broad and final analysis, it would seem that when the President's Commission got out of character and attempted to *investigate and solve,* which it did with the mystery of the bullets, it came a cropper. The Commission's greatest single blunder would seem to be its writing down its "puzzlement" for all to see — and criticize.

To tell our second story, the reader will have to change from the position of a disinterested (and probably confused) observer of a national controversy to that of a participant in a straight-line investigation of the mystery left unsolved by the President's Commission, again the mystery of the bullets. This change will require a nearly diametric shift in the reader's direction of viewing and a revision of his idea of procedural techniques.

In Part III, the reader will be asked to change his direction of viewing from that necessarily taken by the President's Commission to that of an investigator setting out under directive to determine the specific happenings that caused President John F. Kennedy to be shot to death and Governor John B. Connally, Jr., to be grievously wounded by a rifle bullet.

We shall see that for the true investigator, this direction of viewing is outward from the very center of the

64

climactic situation — outward from the most central point of the acts of violence themselves. Outward yes, but only so far as the individual clue, the piece of evidence, the eyewitness account, remains relevant, material, and bears upon the single detail immediately under investigation.

The reader's idea of procedural technique will have to change with respect to gathering and assessing material evidence and testimony. Where the Commission had to review the total circumstance with its innumerable ramifications, we will find ourselves operating within much narrower limits. Where the Commission had to evaluate all possibilities and alternatives, we will first establish *investigative control* and then, using it, we will sift out and assess only pertinent evidence and testimony that relates directly to the shooting episode of the assassination. We can give no time or investigative effort to looking into the many, many things that people see, hear, and imagine, when they try to recall and equate their own reactions, as chance witnesses, to such a shocking instant in time and history. Figuratively speaking, we will trade binoculars for a good strong magnifying glass.

No one questions the fact that the President's Commission did a prodigious job of accumulating about all the data, evidence, and testimony that relates, in any way, to the whole tragic affair. This will prove to be a great boon to us as investigators. We will make good use of this voluminous compilation of facts, figures, theories, and evaluations — provided each item taken from it meets our rigid tests to determine its admissability as evidence.

Later in Chapter VIII, we shall see that even a student investigator with a suitable background of *technical experience* can solve the mystery of the bullets with no more than the material contained in a paperback copy[1] of the official Report; the eyewitness accounts of four persons riding in the presidential limousine;[2] and the pictorial information contained in the Zapruder film sequence (and blowups) pictured in the 25 November 1966 issue of *Life Magazine*.

> Author's Comment: It was arranged this way and with these particular references for three reasons. First, these publications are available to everyone at public libraries or they can be obtained at nominal cost. Second, they contain a great deal of additional evidence, testimony, and general data that can be used to further corroborate and substantiate the solution to the mystery of the bullets contained herein. Third, if the reader is interested in going further into the Government's case, he can continue the investigation on his own and determine for himself whether or not the President's Commission established a case against the man it indicted as an assassin — once it is proved that there was *only one assassin.*

------

[1] Previously cited. *Report of the Warren Commission on the Assassination of President Kennedy.* Bantam Books, Inc., published in October, 1964.

[2] The official verbatim testimony of Mrs. John F. Kennedy, Governor and Mrs. John B. Connally, Jr., and Secret Service Agent Roy H. Kellerman, as interrogated by the Commission. Accurately recorded in *The Witnesses* — Bantam Books, Inc., published in December, 1964.

Chapter VII

AN EXPERIENCED LOOK AT CRITICAL FACTORS

The story of the mystery that has enshrouded the assassination of President John F. Kennedy and the wounding of Governor John B. Connally, Jr., bears out the old saying that truth is stranger than fiction.

Viewed in retrospect, it proves to be a case involving extremes rather than norms. The laws of probability seem to have been suspended, and the normal and expected order of things seems, somehow, to have become unregulated. All good evidence is compromised, all good clues lead away from, rather than towards, the solution, and an unseen force (and a road sign) seems to have purposely blocked out or hidden the keys to a clear-cut solution. All who have tried to solve the central mystery using the face value of the evidence seem to suffer the same fate, and the dilemma, of the President's Commission.

As previously stated, it would not have been solved by the author had not personal experience provided certain data and information that proved to be key or critical in establishing the line of reasoning and the deductive steps that led to the solution of the mystery. These factors are presented here, in some detail, to afford the reader a similar premise.

Military tactics, techniques, and equipment will be seen to figure heavily in this case. We have a bolt-action rifle mounted with a sniper's telescopic sight, full metal-jacketed "Geneva Convention" type bullets, wounds caused by this type of bullet, and a *planned ambush,* one of the deadliest of military tactics.

In the light of the above, the author early suspected that the rifleman who fired upon the presidential limousine from the sixth-floor window of the Texas School Book Depository might have had military rifle marksmanship training.

Due to a lifetime of association, the author is familiar with these things many times over — more than likely the reader is not. In order for the reader to join with the author in this investigation, he must acquire a suitable background of technical experience with these things. Hence, a look at the following:

The Locale and *modus operandi*

The Weapon

The Bullets

The Wounds

Key Witnesses

Bullet Combinations

The Zapruder Movie Film

The Single Bullet Theory

The Locale and *modus operandi*

One of the first moves of a trained investigator is to put himself technically into the shoes of likely suspects.

In this instance, the author not only could place himself at the sixth-floor window of the Book Depository with a scope-mounted bolt-action military rifle resting familiarily in his hands but, by virtue of training and experience, could pretty well visualize and determine the technical planning that would have had to be done beforehand by the assassin. Nor was it difficult to estimate the degree of mental and athletic readiness required of the assassin to aim, fire, and manipulate the bolt-action rifle in the very few seconds available to him.

> Author's Comment: No inference is intended, nor should one be drawn, that the author could entertain, in any shape or form, the twisted mental attitude or thoughts that motivated or prompted the assassin to perpetrate such a terrible deed. Nor is the inference intended or to be drawn that military training would motivate or predispose any person to commit such a crime.

We reconnoiter —

The southside windows of the Texas School Book Depository overlook Dealey Plaza where three of the principal streets of downtown Dallas narrow closer together and go into a triple underpass beneath some railroad switch tracks. Elm Street is the northernmost of these streets.

When dignitaries are in parade escort through downtown Dallas, a usual outbound route for the motorcade is west on Main Street to Houston Street, then right on Houston Street to Elm Street. Beginning at this intersection, Elm

Street passes parallel to the south face of the Depository Building and then continues southwestward down a very shallow decline which makes a gentle "S" curve to the left and then right again before going into a triple underpass several hundred yards down from the Depository.

The sixth floor of the Depository has a large window low to the floor near the southeast corner of the building. This window has all of Dealey Plaza in view as do the other windows on the south face of the building but, uniquely, it commands a straightaway view down the center lane of Elm Street for approximately one hundred yards as it goes downgrade toward the underpass.

The first thing that would strike a field-trained military man as he looked out the sixth-floor window at this straightaway below is the almost out-of-the-training-manual suitability that this vantage point has for setting up an ambush! In the old days, military instructors would say, "Get a concealed position where you can see the enemy coming and going but where they can't see you while they're coming. Don't ever open fire at them coming at your position because they will sense your position and immediately return your fire — wait until they have gone past and are leaving you straightaway. This simplifies your aiming problem and prevents counterfire, because they don't know where your fire is coming from." A modern-day military instructor would undoubtedly add, "And if they are in open vehicles, all the better, because after you open fire, they have no alternative but to try to escape right down your line of fire."

This sixth-floor window of the Texas School Book Depository is, indeed, a unique location from which to fire a high powered rifle at a person sitting in an open limousine slowly going straightaway down Elm Street to the southwest. Except for the thin top branches of an oak tree that

70

interferes with the view of Elm Street for about 55 yards, the line-of-aim is unobstructed and stays essentially fixed for about 135 feet, from 55 yards out to about 95 yards out, requiring only a slight change in sighting elevation as the vehicle (target) moves away toward the Triple Underpass.

Its very uniqueness serves to identify the type of person who would contrive to use it for such a dastardly purpose. First, this person would have had to be physically in position at this particular window to see its unique suitability and, even when there, would not see its true potential unless he had handled high powered rifles and was familiar with their accuracy and lethal effect. Obviously, these qualifications fit a great number of trained riflemen and sportsmen. The cruel twist of fate was its bringing a potential presidential assassin up to gaze out of this window who, by training was qualified to recognize the death-dealing capability of a high powered rifle fired from this vantage point. Once it was found by such a person (and, indeed, it was), the carrying out of the assassination was simply a matter of elementary planning — and opportunity.

What were the planning problems, once the potential assassin decided to commit the deed?

> There might be a little trouble getting the rifle into the building but most rifles can be broken down and packaged to look like something else.
> Shooting from a seated position with an arm rest would be advisable. This would be no problem; there were stacks of boxes and cartons everywhere around. They could be used also to wall off the window from the rest of the sixth floor without raising suspicion.
> The window would have to be opened from the bottom. No problem here; it was opened routinely for ventilation.

71

The top branches of the tree would pose no serious aiming problem. A moving target can be tracked right on through thin branches with a telescopic sight without any loss of aim — just remember not to shoot until the tree is out of the way.

Getting into position unobserved and being ready when the motorcade nears should be no problem. Stockchasers (clerks) are the only Depository employees who frequent the upper floors where they fill orders for books and deliver them by elevator to the shipping section downstairs. Stockchasers move at random on the upper floors and are unsupervised and unobserved most of the time.

The matter of a getaway will be a little more difficult. The rifle will have to be abandoned, but it should not be too hard to get out of the building unnoticed in the confusion that is bound to result.

Other problems such as harmonization of the telescopic sight and practice with the bolt-action rifle will have to be worked out elsewhere. However, practice aiming and tracking (dry firing) can be accomplished anytime one is at the sixth-floor window — there is a never ending stream of vehicles rolling down the Elm Street straightaway on which to practice.

The Weapon

The Military Rifle Itself

There is ample material evidence to establish that a bolt-action Mannlicher-Carcano military rifle mounted with a 4-power telescopic sight was fired at the presidential limousine from the sixth-floor window of the Texas School Book Depository Building — during the assassination.

The Carcano is a high powered, 6.50m/m, clip-fed military rifle manufactured for and used (at one time) by several European armies. This "scope-mounted" rifle is very similar to the type now used by most American sports-

72

men for hunting deer and other large game animals; in fact, it is being purchased in the U.S. principally for this purpose. Although it is relatively inexpensive, as hunting rifles go, it is extremely accurate up to several hundred yards and has all the killing power required for any large game found in the continental United States.

The Telescopic Sight

The telescopic (optical) gunsight eliminates the old "iron sights" bug-a-boo of having to maintain front and rear sight alignment while simultaneously trying to hold the aim on the target. Sight alignment is built into the optics of the telescopic sight. The only aiming required is to place the crosshairs, seen in the optical field of the sight, on the target. Four-power means that the target appears somewhat larger in the scope than it does when viewed with the naked eye. Another way to put it is that objects appear somewhat closer when viewed through a telescopic sight. Most people are familiar with binoculars which operate on the same principle in each eye tube.

The scope-mounted rifle becomes a precision instrument once the line of sighting is harmonized with the line of flight of the bullet.[1] All military riflemen are taught how to "sight in" or harmonize their sights without test-firing the rifle on an outdoor firing range. This procedure is called bore sighting, and amounts to no more than sighting through the bore or barrel of the rifle at a distant aiming point and holding it so aligned, while mechanically adjusting the crosshairs in the scope, until they are on the same distant aiming point as the barrel. Of course, it is preferable to harmonize the sight by test-firing each adjustment at a target on an outdoor range.

Riflemen are in universal agreement that the telescopic

sight is many times easier to aim, especially at slow-moving targets, than any of the many other types of "iron" sights. Properly harmonized, the scope-mounted rifle is a precision instrument that even a beginner can use effectively with only limited practice. To entertain any idea that this weapon was not up to what it was called upon to do, that it was *a rattling piece of useless junk,* as it has been described by several critics, is to be seriously misguided and dangerously misinformed. So long as a cartridge will chamber, lock, and fire in a military rifle, it is a lethal apparatus. With a harmonized telescopic sight, it is a precision instrument that will deal death well out beyond 500 yards.

The Faulty Criterion

The Commission's investigators had the rifle at hand and they had ample proof that it had been fired three times at the President in a very brief span of time — but they ran into serious difficulty, in fact, they ended up in a dilemma trying to answer the simple question of how it was aimed, fired, operated (reloaded), and fired again by the assassin in such a brief span of time.

As touched on in Chapter V, they made the fundamental error early in their deliberations of allowing an assumption to turn into a rigid criterion. The assumption was that the shots that hit the President *had to be well-aimed shots.* From this obviously faulty assumption developed the rigid criterion that the Mannlicher-Carcano rifle could not be fired effectively unless there was an interval of at least 2.3 seconds between consecutive shots.

How did this come about?

Apparently, several Federal Agencies, acting on their own initiative (or at the Commission's request), entered into

74

field tests to determine how rapidly well-aimed shots could be fired using the bolt-action Carcano or a similar type military rifle.

As the assassin had hit the President with 2 out of 3 shots (according to the Commission) at distances varying from 55 yards to 90 yards, well-aimed came to mean essentially that — 2 out of 3 hits in about a 10-inch bull's-eye of a target moving through the distances indicated and within a time lapse of no more than 6 to 7 seconds. NOTE: The points of entry of the President's visible head and neck wounds were about 10 inches apart, hence the author's estimate that a 10-inch bull's-eye was used.

Using various simulations of this marksmanship problem, selected personnel of the Federal Bureau of Investigation and the U.S. Ballistic Research Laboratory fired numerous range tests trying, apparently, to equal either the assassin's marksmanship or his rate of fire, or both. However tested, their final results indicated that it took a minimum of 2.3 seconds between shots *to equal the assassin's apparent skill.*

The lack of validity or applicability of such staged firing tests can be demonstrated simply by adding another assumption to the test schedule. Let us assume that the two bullets had hit the President one inch apart instead of 10 inches. Our test target, then, to equal the assassin's apparent accuracy, has to have a one-inch bull's-eye instead of a 10-inch bull's-eye. Any shooter knows that it would take hours to hit a one-inch bull's-eye on a moving target at distances varying between 55 and 90 yards — if it were ever done at all. What we have developed here is a near impossible shooting problem, if not an absurdity.

The disturbing effect of such a rigid (and faulty) criterion on the logical reasoning processes is seen throughout Chapter III of the official Report. Actually, no clear pattern emerges as to the application given this criterion that at least 2.3 seconds were required to properly aim and fire subsequent shots. It seems that if a subsequent bullet struck the President, the assassin was automatically allotted at least 2.3 seconds of reloading and aiming time. If he missed with a subsequent shot, it was judged (using the criterion) that he had not had his allotted reloading and aiming time. If two shots were fired in less than 2.3 seconds, then the second shot was automatically judged a miss — and so forth and so on, ad dilemma.

The errors and inconsistencies that result when reasoning with such faulty and inapplicable criteria are obvious.

Along with knowing that rigid criteria should never be premised on mere assumptions, experienced investigators know that this type of test data should be used sparingly and applied only in its broadest limits. Properly conducted tests would have first determined that the Carcano rifle could be mechanically reloaded and fired as fast as one shot per second, no aim involved, but that it could not be operated and fired to meet the *specified accuracy* at an interval of less than 2.3 seconds between shots.

The only controlling criterion to be gained from all of the above is that *not more than one shot can be fired per second under any circumstances* — and even this would be used cautiously by experienced investigators.

Why, then, did the Commission's investigators adopt such a faulty and inapplicable criterion? Probably for no other reasons than it was given to them by reputable ballistic agencies of the Federal Government, and, obviously, it had a certain ring of validity — to evaluators.

The point long belabored here is that it is not possible to investigatively determine how the rifle was aimed, operated, and fired by the assassin if the 2.3 seconds between shots criterion (which has no relevancy whatsoever) is used as a controlling factor.

The Reloading Cycle

As to the bolt-action reloading cycle of the Carcano rifle, it is manufactured with low-fitting tolerances (looseness of operating parts) which actually permits the bolt mechanism to be operated easier, and therefore at faster reloading speeds, than similar American-built rifles with tighter fitting parts. Repeated working of the bolt action through its full cycle will cause the parts to wear-in, which tends to loosen the action even further.

Years ago, the author, an Expert Rifleman, using the old iron-sighted, bolt-action U.S. Army Springfield rifle, could fire five rounds (starting with one cartridge chambered) in 6 seconds demonstrating rapid firing techniques to troops under field instruction. To put all 5 shots on an 8 ft. by 8 ft. range target at 100 yards was considered good shooting. Experimenting today with a bolt-action 30-06 sporting rifle with a 4-power telescopic sight, the author can still manage to fire 5 rounds in 7 seconds and put 4 out of 5 shots in a 2-foot circle at 100 yards. *Such is the great advantage of the telescopic sight.*

Aiming and Accuracy

What we finally arrive at is that, with the actual impact points of the assassin's bullets on record (the autopsy), the manner and method by which the Carcano rifle was aimed and fired, whether well-aimed, snapped off, flinched off, or hip shot, is after the fact, a *fait accompli,* and is therefore immaterial in this investigation. The only operating data required in this case is how fast was it humanly possible

77

for the assassin to mechanically work the bolt mechanism of the Carcano rifle and snap off subsequent shots — and the author would put this at about *one shot per second.*

Hard as it may be for even an experienced investigator to accept, the strong possibility exists — and must be considered — that the assassin, under the terrific stress of the moment, either intentionally or by flinching, fired a subsequent shot as he came back on the trigger after having operated the bolt mechanism as rapidly as was physically and mechanically possible.

Assassin's Probable Actions

With all of the foregoing in mind, a reasonable answer to the question, "How was the Carcano rifle aimed, operated, and fired by the assassin?" could be as follows:

The assassin, from a box-seated, arm-rested position (possibly using a hasty sling), probably well-aimed the first shot by tracking the President through the thin top branches of the oak tree (easily done with a telescopic sight) and squeezed off the trigger just as the President came clear of the branches. He then rapidly reloaded[2] and fast-squeezed (or possibly snapped or flinched off) the second shot as the crosshairs came back on the President's general outline. He then reloaded reflexively, and with the range increasing and the scope image decreasing in size, put the crosshairs back on the single image that the President and Mrs. Kennedy were making by that time, tracked momentarily, and steadily squeezed off the final shot. He then reloaded reflexively (a live round was found in the chamber of the Carcano) but, for reasons that can only be surmised, did not fire this last *chambered* cartridge.

The fact of this last chambered, but unfired, cartridge

and the assassin's *apparent* accuracy with two of the three bullets that he did fire, indicate to the author that he aimed all four rounds but did not fire the last one for lack of a good aim or, possibly, if he was a trained rifleman, he could not bring himself to just throw away a last shot.

Estimate of Timing and Accuracy

The elapsed time between the first and second shots, if executed as above, would be from 1 to 1½ seconds; between the second and third shots, 4 seconds, give or take ½ of a second. Minimum total elapsed time — 4.5 seconds; maximum elapsed time — 6 seconds.

A technical analysis of the probable accuracy of each shot, if fired as above, would be as follows. The first shot would have been the only unhurried, well-aimed shot and it was fired at the shortest range — about 58 yards. The possibility of a hit with No. 1 bullet is very high. The second shot was fast-squeezed or snapped off as the crosshairs centered back on the President's image, range about 68 yards. The probability of a hit with No. 2 bullet is only fair to poor. The element of luck becomes a factor but with the telescopic sight — the shooter is favored. The third shot, with the range extending out to 90 yards, was tracked momentarily and squeezed off. This gives a fair to good probability of a hit with sight harmonization becoming a critical factor.

If a trained rifleman were to attempt the same three shots a dozen times with the same order of firing, it is a reasonable estimate that he would hit with the first shot every time, miss with the second shot 7 times out of 12, and hit with the third shot 6 times out of 12.

If the asssassin hit 3 out of 3 the first go around (we will

79

find out in Chapter VIII that he did), this proves to be better than average shooting — *for the second shot only!*

Could he manipulate the bolt-action Carcano rifle according to the minimum time schedule? Yes, but with reloading and aiming difficulty on the second shot. According to the maximum time schedule? Yes, and with improved accuracy all around. Could he hit effectively at this reloading and aiming rate? This is the investigative question that answers itself; the record (the wounds he inflicted) demonstrates that he did — and even more effectively, we shall see, than the President's Commission determined.

Two things will never be determined: the assassin's intended aiming point on the President's optical image — and the amount of luck involved with all three shots.

> Ballistic Note: The built-in sight harmonization error in the Carcano of 6 to 8 inches high and to the right (footnote 1) would have a continuing effect on all shots as would the requirement to lead the target in the direction that it appeared (to the shooter) to be moving. It would have been rising slowly in his field of view and drifting slightly to the right. Without getting too technical, it can be said that the harmonization error just about compensated for the lead or aimoff that this moving target required. If the shooter put on lead or aimoff, not knowing of his harmonization error, he would tend, on the average, to miss his intended aiming point slightly high and to the right.

The Bullets

Specifications

An unexpended cartridge was found in the chamber of the Mannlicher-Carcano rifle. It cased a 6.50m/m, 160 grain blunt-nosed, full metal-jacketed bullet that, ironically enough, complies with International Accords insofar as its *humane* wounding effects are concerned. Opposed to this humane bullet is the modern sportsman's *expanding* or *mushrooming* bullet designed to do just that, spread on impact. The Expander makes a normal bullet hole on entering but blows out a hole the size of a fist on exiting. The humane full metal-jacketed bullet, on the other hand, passes through clean and exits through a hole not much larger than its entrance hole — provided no bone is struck that would cause the bullet to lose its pristine characteristic.

Ballistic Note: *Pristine characteristic* is a condition of ballistic stability in a bullet in streamlined, high-velocity flight due to the gyroscopic spin around its flight axis imparted to it by the rifling in the barrel of the gun. This spin rate must be exceedingly high (120-130,000 revolutions per minute out of the Carcano rifle) to insure that gyroscopic *rigidity in space* characterics are set up in the bullet so that it will hold to a very uniform, and therefore aimable, flight path through the air.

All bullets, high and low velocity alike, and full-jacketed bullets more so than others, tend to ricochet or glance off any object or surface that they strike at an angle (tangentially) in their highspeed course. This ricochetting or glancing effect is purely a matter of physical dynamics. The skipping action of a flat stone cast out over a calm water surface is a common example of ricochet action.

There was strong evidence to prove that only full-jacketed bullets had been fired. One, almost intact, was found under such circumstances as to indicate that it had caused Governor Connally's multiple wounds and had ended up, spent, in his clothing. Two large bullet fragments, one identifiable as a nose section and the other a tail or base section, were found in the driver's compartment of the presidential limousine. There were other nondescript fragments found on the rug under Mrs. Connally's jump seat in the rear compartment of the limousine. The whole bullet and the two major fragments showed, by conclusive ballistic tests, that they had all been fired by the Carcano rifle. There was no ballistic way of determining if the two large fragments represented one bullet or two bullets.

Relative Wind

Both large fragments having been found in the front compartment of the presidential limousine is significant to an investigator. The bullet that penetrated the rear of the President's head and generated the massive head wound was not found in the wound at the autopsy. It is to be remembered that this was the last shot that visibly hit the President and that the limousine was at a speed in excess of the calculated average speed of 11.2 mph as it was gaining speed as it rolled downgrade through the straightaway towards the Triple Underpass. In other words, there was a *relative wind* blowing over the open limousine from front to rear of some 12 to 15 miles per hour due to its road speed. A good pre-investigation guess would be that the bullet very likely fragmented in the President's head and was blown out of the massive wound with brain matter and parts of the skull — with the resulting fragments retaining a good bit of the striking velocity of the whole bullet. Tending as they would to continue on the whole bullet's initial trajectory, they would fly, like birdshot fired into the wind, somewhere into the area forward of the President in the general direction of the Triple Underpass.

82

Multiple assassin theorists have made much of the fact that skull fragments and brain tissue from the President's massive (and seemingly explosive) head wound appeared to have blown rearward and sideward, supposedly by bullet impact(s), sufficiently to splatter the motorcyclists traveling on the left rear of the presidential limousine and to cause skull fragments to fall to the ground as far out as the south curb of Elm Street.

The phenomenon of light animal matter and tissue *appearing* to blow rearward and sideward relative to the direction of travel of a moving vehicle is easily explained by the action of the so-called "relative wind" that blows from the front to the rear of any vehicle due to its speed down the road.

The simple example of casting a cupful of any light material directly upward into the slip-stream of an open vehicle traveling at 12-15 miles per hour will demonstrate quickly enough what happens — the relative wind sweeps the material rearward into the vortex of swirling air that occurs immediately behind any moving vehicle and literally scatters the material to the four winds. Any natural crosswind that might be blowing at the time adds impetus to the relative wind and causes lateral dispersion of the material in the direction the natural wind is blowing.

The Spent Bullet

We have every indication of the ballistic phenomenon that Governor Connally's multiple wounds were caused by a single bullet and that this bullet ended up spent in his clothing. Reasoning from effect back to cause, there is every ballistic and wound-trauma indication that the bullet hit Governor Connally with a velocity considerably below its computed velocity at the range involved. Looking at it from cause to effect, if this full-jacketed bullet had hit

83

Governor Connally with its computed velocity (at 68 yards), it would have blasted his side more severely, completely shattered his wrist, and continued on, somewhat more deformed, and buried itself in the back of the front seat of the limousine. There even would have been the possibility of its piercing the front seat and injurying Secret Service Agent Roy H. Kellerman, who occupied the seat directly ahead of Governor Connally.

What could have caused this reduction in velocity of a full-jacketed bullet? The answer to this question is plain enough — the President's autopsy disclosed that a bullet had passed clean through his neck from rear to front on a course essentially aligned with Governor Connally's back. It doesn't take a master detective to determine the probable path of the full-jacketed, high-velocity rifle bullet that was found spent in Governor Connally's clothing.

With the foregoing analysis at hand, the Single Bullet Theory would no longer be considered a theory by a competent investigator. He would note and record: one full-jacketed bullet — fired from Carcano rifle — passed clean through President's neck and continued on downward course with reduced velocity to cause Governor Connally's multiple wounds — spent bullet recovered — no ballistic evidence to indicate that incident happened otherwise — whether 1st, 2nd or 3rd bullet fired not determinable at this time.

Bullet Segmentation

We must not overlook another investigative lead with respect to the President's massive head wound. This final bullet struck the President in the rear portion of his skull, causing a typical entrance wound. We have every indication that it was a full-jacketed bullet. An elongation of

84

the entrance hole along one axis indicates that the bullet had struck the skull surface at a fairly high angle. In other words, it was not at a flat enough angle to cause the bullet to ricochet.

The angle at which a high velocity bullet strikes a bone surface such as the skull plate can be critical in another ballistic respect; it can cause the bullet to break into segments or, as it is more commonly stated, to fragment. The dynamics of high-velocity bullets are too complex to be discussed here, but the segmentation of a full-jacketed bullet can be demonstrated by a simple parallel. If a common lead pencil is stood on end on a hard surface and grasped in the fist like an ice pick, it can be pecked at the surface quite firmly without breaking the pencil. Tilt it 45° to the surface and even gentle attempts to icepick the slanting surface will cause the pencil to break in two just below your lowest grasping finger. This same bending stress occurs within a full-jacketed bullet that strikes a flat surface at an angle. The front end of the bullet wants to glance off the surface (change direction) while the rear segment or base of the bullet wants to keep on going in its original direction. Due to its extremely high velocity and *gyroscopic rigidity* along its flight path, momentary internal stresses are set up within the bullet itself at the instant it strikes the surface, which cause it to segment or sectionalize. Further fragmentation then results from a disruptive collision between the nose and base segments. An experienced investigator would suspect segmentation in this case because of the fairly high striking angle indicated.

Up to the point of striking the President, this full-jacketed bullet had demonstrated a typical ballistic pattern. If it had continued typically, it probably would have exited through the front portion of his skull, causing a fairly large but not expansive exit wound, or it could have

85

been deflected interiorly downward and spent itself (its fragments) in the dense tissue of the lower brain case — but it did neither. It entered typically, segmented, and then literally blew out with the President's brains through a massive hole in the top of his head.

"Confined Liquid" and "Jet Propulsion" Effect

In technical parlance, such a "blowout" effect would be described as the "confined liquid effect" of a high-velocity bullet.[3] This effect is nothing more nor less than the workings of a law of physics that we all learned in high school. *Paschal's Law* states that, "Any external force exerted on a unit of area in a confined liquid is transmitted undiminished to every unit of area of the interior of the container." The hydraulic jack is a common example of the transmission of pressure through a liquid in a closed container.

To a rifleman, the more common example is the explosive or bursting effect that occurs when a high powered rifle bullet is fired into a closed semi-rigid container completely filled with an incompressible liquid. Shoot a high-velocity bullet into say an unopened No. 10 can of tomatoes and the violence of the explosion can be extremely dangerous to anyone within a radius of 30 feet or more. What causes this? The bullet enters the can and displaces liquid volumetrically, thus increasing the pressure at the point of entry into the can which, according to *Pascal's Law,* is transmitted undiminished to the entire interior surface of the can. The violence of the reaction (explosion) is due to the speed of the bullet, which displaces the liquid at a lineal rate of nearly 2,000 feet per second.

Another phenomenon growing out of this same reaction or explosion is the "jet propulsion" effect. If a high-velocity bullet is fired into a closed container filled with a liquid and there is a weak spot in the container, it will burst explosively, but the initial pressure buildup will force liquid to blow out or jet out of the weak spot first, which, as it occurs, will force the container to move by jet propulsion in the direction opposite to the liquid jetting out through the weak spot.

Both "confined liquid" bursting effect and "jet propulsion" effect can be demonstrated (pick a safe place) by firing a high-velocity hunting rifle bullet into a one gallon plastic bottle completely filled with water that has had its spout opening sealed over with some very thin material such as wax paper. No matter where the bottle is hit, provided the bullet penetrates the bottle, it will always move away from the spout (the weak spot) while blowing to pieces. If it is shot at while standing with the spout upright, it cannot move downward due to the ground but the water will be seen to geyser unusually high through the spout before the container bursts.

The strongest impression an experienced investigator gets after reviewing the evidence and testimony surrounding the President's massive head wound is that the phenomenon described above might account for such a massive, eviscerative-type head wound, especially when strong evidence indicates that it was inflicted by a high-velocity rifle bullet at under 90 yards range.

The skull case in a living human can be considered a closed container and the blood-filled brain tissue can be considered liquid and essentially incompressible. When considered in relation to the "confined liquid" effect, the human skull with its fully enshrouding scalp and skin tissue is usually resilient enough to withstand the momentary displacement pressures without bursting, especially when the bullet has lost part of its initial velocity in travelling 80 to 90 yards and after penetrating the skull bone on entering.

Mechanically speaking, the human scalp, when intact, completely encases the skull as a tire casing encases the inner tube of a pneumatic tire. This encasement contributes considerable resistance to any internal pressure trying to burst open the skull case. *It can be said that an opening in the scalp is tantamount to a weak spot in the skull itself.*

Investigators experienced with the varied phenomena of high-velocity bullets would be on the watch for something that might have weakened the President's skull case or otherwise disrupted its enshrouding scalp — at some time prior to the final wound.

The Sounds of Bullets

The sounds made by bullets are a study in themselves. It is interesting to note that the average person has never heard the sound of a bullet. He has heard the sound (report) of the weapon that fires the bullet and, more than likely, has heard the sound of a target being struck by a bullet.

A high-velocity bullet traveling streamlined through the air generates a shock wave which is a very distinct sound to the human ear. For those who have not heard a high-velocity bullet passing close by, it sounds like a small firecracker or a very loud snap of the fingers. The closer it passes to you, the louder the snap.

A cardinal rule to follow when investigating high powered rifle shots it to identify the bullet *snap* and the rifle *report* as separate sounds where possible and then try to pair them back together again ballistically, using the sound and bullet velocity differential. The ballistic rule to keep in mind is that a high-velocity bullet travels 2 to 3 times faster through the air than does the sound generated by the rifle firing the bullet. As they both start from the same place, the bullet obviously runs away from its own rifle report.

A few old soldiers' rules have good investigative application in the case at point:

— The old saying that you never hear the shot (rifle report) that kills you is to say, simply, that the bullet gets there first. If a soldier is hit between the eyes at 500 yards, he is dead before the rifle report has traveled *even half way to him* from the rifleman who shot him to death.

— It is unlikely that you will hear the rifle report of a bullet that hits you hard (but doesn't kill you) because your bodily attention is on another sensing network — and you are already hurting when the sound of the rifle report gets to your ear.

— You hear a rifle report more clearly and with less resonance and echo effect if you are close to the line the bullet is traveling.

— If the bullet misses you and snaps overhead or strikes nearby, wait for the rifle report and try to locate the rifleman by orienting on the sound of the following rifle report — *do not orient on the snap.*

— The farther you are away from the rifleman, the longer the interval between the snap of the bullet overhead and the following rifle report.

— As you get closer to the rifleman, the snap of the bullet overhead and the rifle report get closer together until, at very short range, they become a combined sound.

— If you are foxholed or entrenched, the snap of the

bullet passing overhead intensifies while the somewhat blanked-off sound of the rifle report diminishes or muffles.

A ricochetting or glancing bullet may take on a variety of sounds, depending on the amount the bullet is deflected off its line of flight and the amount of disruption to its gyroscopic (pristine) characteristic. This can vary from no effect at all, through a whining sound to a screaming whine, and finally, when the bullet loses its gyroscopic stability (while still at high velocity) and starts to wobble or tumble end over end, it changes into a rapidly pulsating whine that sounds like a Chinese pinwheel. Fragmenting ricochets make sounds that defy description.

Hearing, itself, is one of the best recognizing senses that the human has but, unquestionably, it is the poorest accounting sense. The ear does a good job of reporting what it sounded like to the listener but it runs into difficulty as soon as it is asked to remember, "How many? How loud? At what interval? What exact words?" And, when echoes are involved, "What direction?"

The ear, unfortunately, has to hear (listen to) all sounds and contemporary noises simultaneously and then rely on the audio center in the brain to tune up the sound that it thinks the listener is trying to hear — while filtering out or dampening the others. Another difficulty is that the aural sense is usually overridden by one or more of the other senses in climactic or shocking circumstances. This is especially true when the eyes are intent on something other than that which is creating the sound — or the body's nervous system suffers systemic shock or pain sensations from injury.

Experienced investigators learn early to discount "ear testimony," or disregard it entirely unless it can be corroborated on a concensus basis or on a mechanical measuring or recording basis, if such means are available.

The Wounds

The Soldier's Categorization

Doctors, necessarily, must relate bullet wounds to the physical injury that is done to the victim; investigators, on the other hand, must relate the wounds back to the bullet or bullets that caused them. Due to this requirement, the investigator finds it more practical to use the field soldier's categorization of battle wounds rather than the doctor's exceedingly complex system.

Starting from your outline or the silhouette you present as a target and working inward, you can be:

Creased — the bullet slides by on the surface and only abrades the skin or exposed tissue.

Laced — the bullet passes along just under the skin causing an open gash.

Shallow-laced — the bullet goes near bone that is close to the body surface and then glances off. Skin and covering flesh are slashed or ploughed open. Typical of scalp and shoulder blade areas; usually attended with mild concussive effects and possible hairline-type fractures where bone is touched.

Deep-laced —the bullet goes straight to bone but immediately glances off or ricochettes out of the body. Usually attended with severe concussive and bone shattering effects.

Flesh Wound — any of the foregoing with no critical tissue or bone involved.

Deep Penetrating Wound — a variety beyond description.

Multiple Wounds (single bullet) — a variety beyond description but their order of occurrence can usually be determined due to the bullet track and the diminishing wounding effect of the bullet as it loses velocity.

Multiple Wounds (more than one bullet) — a variety that defies description — and an investigator's nightmare. One thing must be borne in mind continually when this type of wound is suspected — subsequent wounds invariably complicate, disguise, or obliterate previous wounds that occurred on or near the same site.

Analysis of Inflicted Wounds

A trained investigator would note the wounds in the case at point as follows:

Governor Connally's multiple wounds — single bullet continuity and diminishing velocity effect evident. Back wound — deep lace of the rib cage with attendant bone shattering effect — bullet continued on. Wrist wound — direct penetrating type evidencing relatively low velocity with respect to bone shattering effect — bullet continued on. Thigh wound — shallow flesh wound evidencing spent bullet effect. *All wounds indicating bullet velocity below that computed for this type of cartridge and 160 grain bullet at short range (about 68 yards).*

President Kennedy's neck wound — penetrating flesh wound — bullet passed clean through his neck from back to front. Probably not lethal, very likely would have prevented President from uttering intelligible sounds due to damage to his larynx (voice box). Passage through the President's back and neck tissue would have reduced bullet velocity but would not have diverted course of bullet materially. Wound obviously caused by a full metal-jacketed high-velocity bullet. Bullet would inflict material damage or cause serious injury to anything struck on its continuing trajectory.

President Kennedy's head wounds — entrance wound — a penetrating wound entering brain after having penetrated skull at an angle sufficiently high to preclude ricochet, but low enough to induce segmentation (breakup) of a full metal-jacketed bullet moving at high velocity. Exit wound — excessive, considering range and indications that bullet was full metal-jacketed. "Confined liquid effect" indicated but improbable — unless the result of a *multiple wound* condition.

Bullet Penetration

Autopsy disclosed that a bullet had struck the President from behind in the neck-shoulder area of the back and that the first tissue penetrated was the musculature which is attached to and which articulates the shoulder blade (scapula).

The argument has been advanced by some critics that because the path (tunnel) of this bullet through the President's body could not be determined by direct probing of the wound, *that it could not be established that a bullet had passed through his neck.*

This argument disregards an anatomical feature of the human body and also the penetrating power of a full metal-jacketed high-velocity rifle bullet.

The anatomical feature is that the shoulder blade and its attached musculature float on the back of the rib cage through a wide range in the plane of the back. A bullet, first passing through the tissue of a shoulder blade and then continuing on through relatively fixed tissue such as the neck tissue, is bound to have its pathway disrupted (and lose its continuity) when the shoulder blade and its surrounding tissue shifts to any other position on the back. The *least likely phenomenon to occur* would be for the wound to retain its tunnel continuity through these sliding and shifting tissues.

There is no problem here for the trained investigator as regards bullet penetration or its capacity to pass through 6 to 8 inches of flesh and cartilage. If an entrance wound is found for a high-velocity bullet and the bullet is not found in the tissue — it passed through! If the exit wound is a gaping hole, it was a "mushrooming" bullet or there will be evidence that a full metal-jacketed bullet struck bone and either lost its pristine characteristic or fragmented before exiting. If the bullet traversed considerable tissue and the exit wound is small, the ballistic indication is that it was a full-jacketed bullet piercing at relatively high velocity.

NOTE: The investigative significance of the path of this bullet through the President's neck will not be seen until later in our investigation when it is considered in relation to his physical posture and his anatomical alignments at the time he was struck.

Partial Penetration Theory

An unusual theory, which runs counter to the concept that a bullet from the Carcano rifle passed clean through the President's neck (counter to The Single Bullet Theory also), is that this same bullet struck the President in the back (point first) but penetrated the tissue only so far as would allow it to be worked back out its small entrance hole when, at Parkland Hospital, the President was given exterior heart massage, along with other heroic medical measures, in an effort to sustain life. This theory necessarily presupposes that the shallow penetration of the bullet

94

resulted from low bullet velocity which, according to the theory, resulted from its having been fired from a defective cartridge with a low powder charge.

A trained investigator would reject this theory on the basis that it is a ballistic impossibility to shoot *even an abnormally aimed* bullet out of a rifled barrel at a target 50-60 yards away and (1) have it hit point first and (2) then have it make only a shallow penetration of human tissue.

The controlling factor here is the bullet's velocity which, to meet the shallow penetration requirements, would have to be reduced from its normal muzzle velocity of some 2,000 feet per second to a muzzle velocity of no more than 150 feet per second.

It follows that a muzzle velocity of only 150 feet per second (only a little above the starting speed of a fast baseball pitch) simply will not impart sufficient pristine characteristic (gyroscopic spin) to the bullet to permit it to establish a stable flight path after it emanates from the muzzle of the rifle. Ballistically speaking, the bullet would be essentially unaimable due to its inherent instability as a missile and its resulting erratic, and therefore unpredictable, trajectory.

Ballistic Note: Even as little as 10 to 15 percent reduction in muzzle velocity (reduced powder charge) will cause erratic and unpredictable bullet flight which, as a consequence, makes the bullet unaimable, even at relatively high velocities.

Suffice it to say that the reader could throw the bullet more accurately and about as far as the Carcano would pitch it (end over end) if it came out of the muzzle of the rifle with no pristine characteristic and traveling at only 150 feet per second.

Key Witnesses

As will be seen in Chapter VIII, the only testimony used to solve the mystery of the bullets comes from the eyewitness accounts of the persons riding in the presidential limousine. These persons were the President (a silent witness) and Mrs. Kennedy, Governor and Mrs. Connally, and Secret Service Agent Roy H. Kellerman. With this being the case, it will be the eternal embarrassment of the President's Commission that it used their collective testimony so poorly. The President's spoken words were never used as evidence and his silent (pictorial) testimony was misconstrued. Governor Connally was not believed, and Mrs. Connally was thought to have been unduly influenced by her husband's story. Though interrogated deferentially (and long after the assassination), Mrs. Kennedy's testimony was all but ignored. Secret Service Agent Kellerman was thought to have been imagining things.

In deference to their stations and their feelings, these individuals were interrogated by senior members of the Commission. Judging from the questions put to these key witnesses, there can be little doubt but that the interrogators were much influenced by their own preconceived notions and theories as to what had transpired. Against the considerable pressure of disbelief, Governor and Mrs. Connally stood their separate ground throughout all questioning (and cross-examination) and have kept on telling it as they saw and heard it.

Mrs. Kennedy, admitting to the interrogators that she had read of their notions and theories beforehand, tried valiantly to tell it as she had experienced it, but finally was overwhelmed (with doubt) and ended up agreeing that she was mixed up between what she had remembered originally — and what she had been led to believe.

Agent Kellerman told a clear straight story (in his vernacular) of what actually had occurred. His testimony was simply disregarded.

It would appear that the Commission, upon finding that these eyewitness accounts did not jibe with their preconceived notions and theories, either disqualified or disregarded this vital testimony on the basis that the witnesses were too distraught to remember what had happened.

Fortunately for our purposes, the valiant efforts of these witnesses, in trying to tell it as they saw it, is recorded verbatim and provides us, as investigators, with the evidence needed to solve the mystery of the bullets.

It has been the author's experience as an investigator of climactic circumstances that the accounts of witnesses whose utterances and instantaneous reactions are (in legal terms) a part of the *res gestae,* prove very valuable in establishing or identifying key elements of the central circumstance under investigation.

The Latin words *res gestae* translate into English as "things done." When the phrase, "a part of the *res gestae*" is used in legal or investigative work, it applies to things done or uttered by persons in direct, immediate, and reflexive or involuntary reaction to a startling, shocking or greatly disappointing occurrence.

For instance, Governor Connally's ejaculation, "Oh, no, no, no," (as overheard by both Mrs. Connally and Mrs. Kennedy) on his hearing the first rifle shot, and turning instantly to try to locate its source, would be a part of the *res gestae* growing out of the first rifle report.

Mrs. Kennedy's exclamation, "Jack, they have killed my husband," (overheard by Mrs. Connally) on her first seeing the President as Governor Connally caused her to look around by crying "Oh, no, no, no," is also a part of the *res gestae* of the first rifle report.

97

The President's ejaculation, "My God, I am hit," as heard by Secret Service Agent Roy H. Kellerman (sitting in the front seat of the presidential limousine) on turning to the right after hearing the "firecracker, pop" of a bullet overheard, is a part of the *res gestae* of the first rifle report.

An investigative requirement, when working with written testimony, is to translate formally recorded words and expressions back into the most likely phonetic sounds and inflections that would have been put forth by the persons making such utterances. We have already noted that the hearing sense is an excellent recognizing sense but that it leaves much to be desired as a recounting sense. Obviously, there is a wide difference between what is uttered phonetically and inflectionally and what is heard (and understood) by listeners.

As these utterances start suddenly and reflexively, they cannot, by the very nature of their sudden projection, begin with tongued or lipped words of speech. A common example of the reflective utterance is the "OU!" of "ouch" when we voice sudden sharp pain.

For investigators, the *key sound* in a spontaneous ejaculation is the starting or opening sound. The reason for this being that it can be established with reference to a point in time or in a sequence with respect to time lapse. Once established, it then permits other reactions resulting from hearing the start of the utterance to be aligned with time. Often, such utterances are the only evidence available upon which to determine sequential and timetable data.

Governor Connally's ejaculation (from dismay) could have started with "OH!" or possibly "OH!NO!" Mrs. Kennedy's exclamation (on seeing a shocking sight) undoubtedly started with "JACK!" President Kennedy's ejaculation (on having been struck) certainly was not a formal and literal "My — God — I — am — hit." "GOD! I'm hit!" is more likely which probably was phonetically and inflectively ejacuated as "—AWED! mmm..it," with the inflected word "—AWED!" as the starting sound.

The *key words* in utterances of this nature are any that identify or furnish clues as to what brought forth the utterance in the first place. Governor Connally's "no, no, no" is indicative of anguished protest. Mrs. Kennedy simply put a shocking observation (and judgement) into words. President Kennedy voiced surprise and shock — and stated the cause of it!

> Author's Comment: It is a typical and natural failing of witnesses to literalize or grammatically formalize their initial aural impressions of such sudden and fleeting utterances. The tendency to formalize increases with repeated and pointed questioning, especially when the interrogator, consciously or unconsciously, shows skepticism or disbelief. It also increases in an almost direct ratio with the amount of time the witness has had to think over, and mentally reconstruct, the incident — before being properly interrogated.
>
> Another point for the investigator to keep in mind is the reflexive nature of the physical reactions of people hearing such ejaculations and utterances. Fortunately for his safety, the human has retained the greater part of the basic animal capability of turning to see (or escape) any sharp sound or loud ejaculation that startles the auditory nerve channel to the brain. As the reaction (physical movement) is reflexive, it generates far more rapid head, eye and body movements than we can effect voluntarily.

Acts and utterances that can be shown to be a part of the *res gestae* are considered to be strong and weighty evidence by trained investigators. Such evidence is considered strong enough to be admissable in a court of law in its usual form as "hearsay evidence" — which, normally, is not admissible. This rule of evidence stems from the generally held belief that such acts and utterances (whether accurate or not) are spontaneous, involuntary in the most part, and therefore are not influenced by conscious thoughts or mental reservations. A characteristic of utterances that are part of the *res gestae* is that they are seldom accurately remembered by the person who made them. This is also true of physical acts, but to a lesser degree. The reason for this forgetfulness is to be found in the very fact that it is an overriding circumstance that calls them forth in the first place.

As a military commander, the author had, on many occasions, done a similar duty to that which Governor Connally was performing that tragic day in Dallas — escorting a person of high office through the confines of his area of responsibility. There are many things on the mind of a ranking escort official, not the least of which is the ever-present possibility of an attempt to embarrass or harm the high official. Governor Connally's reactions, from the instant he heard the rifle report until he momentarily collected himself after being struck, are typical of a man reacting to official responsibility rather than to pain. This is clearly evident in his utterance the instant after he was struck, "My God, they are going to kill us all!"

When the sharp report of a high powered rifle rang out, Governor Connally was unquestionably (and by his own testimony) among the first to recognize it for what it was — and what it meant! It is understandable that he would utter what he did. Who has not, in dismay, uttered, "Oh, no, no, no," when confronted with the shocking realization that fate has taken over and all that can be done is voice a futile protest.

We shall see that there was one other, even before

Governor Connally, who probably did not hear the shot but recognized it for what it was and voiced its effect. His ejaculation, "God, I'm hit," points unerringly to the key to solving the mystery of the three bullets that hit, and with consolidating effect — killed him!

Bullet Combinations

Inexperienced investigators are inclined to overlook the true complexity of the problems associated with determining bullet combinations and sequences. They fail to see the geometric progression that occurs as the number of bullets fired at a victim increases beyond one.

If one bullet is fired at a man, we have three possibilities; the bullet can miss, wound or kill him. If an autopsy discloses that he died of a bullet wound, and only one bullet was fired, an investigation into the proximal cause of death is hardly required. However, when two bullets are fired at a man, we find ourselves confronted with a number of possible combinations of miss, wound or kill, e.g., we can have two misses, two wounds, two lethal wounds, a miss and a lethal wound, etc. — up to nine possible combinations. Also, the order or sequence of some of these combinations can be changed once, i.e., a miss and a wound can also be a wound followed by a miss.

If the man is wounded or killed by any of the combinations other than two misses, we are now in need of an investigator to determine which combination occurred and in what sequence.

Three bullets fired at a man give us twenty-odd combinations and possible sequences in excess of that. *Three bullets* fired at two men (our case at point) moves us up to fifty-odd combinations and innumerable sequences.

The object lesson here for investigators is that the solu-

101

tion to our mystery lies in determining *two combinations* and their matching sequences (one for President Kennedy and one for Governor Connally) out of innumerable possible combinations and sequences. This tells us that the trained investigator must keep his mind open to all possible combinations and sequences — eliminating them from consideration only when they can be proven to be beyond the realm of possibility.

In the President's case, the Commission selected the combination of miss, wound and kill. In Governor Connally's case, miss, wound and miss. The sequence in which each combination occurred was never fully determined and the only information put out regarding how the two combinations matched was the somewhat veiled statement that, "Very persuasive evidence from the experts . . . " indicated that one bullet may have wounded both men.

Actually, the Commission considered only one combination put in three different sequences. Their treatment of the "miss" can be best shown by chart:

	Original open and shut case (discarded)	Warren Report using "Single Bullet Theory" (SBT) & Bullet that Missed		
		1st comb.	2nd comb.	3rd comb.
1st bullet	Pres-neck	MISSED	Pres-neck Connally	Pres-neck Connally
2nd bullet	Connally	Pres-neck Connally	MISSED	Pres-head (lethal)
3rd bullet	Pres-head (lethal)	Pres-head (lethal)	Pres-head (lethal)	MISSED

102

It is readily apparent from the chart that the controlling factor with the Commission was the bullet that missed. The (SBT) bullet, the one that may have wounded both men, seems to have been somewhat of an unwanted child to the Commission's investigators. According to how they saw it, the SBT bullet had to sequence ahead of the President's lethal head wound and with his neck wound — which just didn't fit with other theories — and preconceptions — held by them.

The chart tells the story of the Commission's failure to solve the mystery of the bullets and its disinclination to factualize the Single Bullet Theory.

For reasons explained in Part II, the Commission's investigators latched on to only one combination for the President and, unfortunately, it was incorrect. This points up one of their fundamental investigative errors: they failed to keep an open mind on possible combinations — and this they did in the face of extensive evidence and testimony (which they had painstakingly gathered) indicating that other combinations should have been explored.

Their dilemma, as explained in Chapter V, resulted from the single fact that the combination they did select — miss, wound and kill — was inherently incorrect — and no amount of sequential juggling could ever put it right.

The Zapruder Moving Picture Film

The motion picture camera is a viewing and surveying instrument of unusual accuracy — but only with respect to certain measurable and mathematically determinable things. This accuracy results from two engineering features of a movie camera, one mechanical and the other optical.

First, the movie camera is a cyclic mechanical device

103

in which a film strip is brought to a complete stop behind a light shutter each time a single picture (frame) is exposed or taken.

The camera used by Mr. Abraham Zapruder of Dallas, Texas, that filmed the entire assassination took individual, consecutive pictures at a cyclic rate of 18.3 picture frames per second. We see, immediately, that we have a basis upon which to measure what investigators call time lapse or, simply the passage of time. Any strip of film containing 18.3 consecutive frames measures one second of time or each frame represents approximately 1/20 of a second of elapsed time.

We see, also, that each individual picture frame, when compared with the preceding and following picture frames, gives an incremental time lapse (1/20 of a second for each interval between consecutive frames), an incremental change in the spatial location (ground position) of moving things, and an incremental change in the movements, animations, and expressions of human beings caught in the camera's view. Being consecutive, these incremental changes give the investigator a basis upon which to perceive, and often measure or calculate, the motions and occurrences of near-instantaneous things and conditions.

The optical feature is that the movie camera, however pointed, views all things through a fixed and unchanging optical alignment — the same as our telescopic rifle sight. The optical axis or direction of the picture is as centered in the individual picture frame.

By combining the mechanical and optical features of a movie camera, we can accurately determine the ground position or spatial location of all objects visible in the camera's field of view. We can measure or determine directions and distances and any change in appearance and position of moving objects, and we can put all these relative

104

to time lapse and sequence of happening. In other words, if the camera can see an object with reasonable clarity, we can identify it, determine its relative position, locate ground points from which we can calculate its rate and direction of movement, and, if animate and reacting, determine the speed and character of the reaction.

To use this evidence properly, the investigator must be apprised of some limitations to camera-eye evidence. An obvious shortcoming is that the Zapruder camera did not record sound. We view a silent movie or we study individual pictures of a scene, one of the overwhelming features of which was the cacophony of sounds and noises that accompanied it.

Compared to the human bifocal view, which facilitates depth perception, the camera sees with a single eye and in a very restricted cone of view. Like the human eye, it cannot see through solid or opaque objects nor can it photograph objects moving at high velocities, such as bullets in flight. It blurs objects moving at intermediate velocities and blurs its whole field of view when jiggled or moved too rapidly while taking a picture. Again, like the human eye, it can fail to focus properly.

All these limitations must be taken into account when using evidence obtainable from this otherwise excellent surveying instrument. Usually, these limitations are self-evident or self-limiting within themselves.

However, there is one investigative limitation to camera-eye evidence that is by no means self-limiting. It could, in fact, be called self-generating because it involves a human or volitional factor. It has to do with reading things into photographs that are not there.

To keep from committing this serious investigative error (photo interpretation error), we must qualify all still evidence and evidence involving the actions and reactions of things (especially human beings) photographed by a movie camera as happening as viewed in the pictures, rather than happening as otherwise suggested, inferred, or qualified by evidence *gathered elsewhere than from the pictures themselves.*

As an example, a determination to the effect that Zapruder film frame No. 313 shows the President getting hit by the bullet that hit him in the back of his head and blew his brains out — would be completely inaccurate. Why is this so? First, the camera cannot photograph a high-velocity bullet in flight so how can it be stated that a bullet hit the President — let alone in the back of the head? Although the camera photographed a substance appearing immediately above the President's head, this does not permit identifying the substance as brain matter.

The only legally (and investigatively) admissible evidence obtainable from this single photograph (film frame No. 313) would be as follows: material, sufficient in density to be photographed, was visible and appeared in the area touching and immediately above the top of the President's head.

What admissible evidence becomes available to us when we consider film frame No. 313 with the immediately preceding and following film frames in the moving picture sequence? Comparison of sequential picture frames shows that the material, sufficient in density to be photographed, appeared instantly (in 1/20 of a second or less), in film frame No. 313 — it was not visible in the preceding frame No. 312 — and continued visible until frame No. 318 several frames later. Comparisons further show that the President's head moved forward perceptibly in the 1/20 of a second between frames 312 and 313 and then made a retro-

106

movement backward and to the left in the 3/20 of a second between frames 313 and 316. Such evidence as the above is factual — and incontestable.

From the above, it should be apparent that the only evidence available from a photograph is what actually can be seen — and this only in its most general condition or sense. Included, of course, is what can be mathematically calculated or determined by sequential comparisons and measurements.

Photo interpretation errors can be considered natural errors because it is the natural human way to associate or tie together what is seen — with what has been learned previously or experienced otherwise. Unfortunately, what is normal everyday practice becomes a serious investigative mistake — when applied to photo interpretation. Just such a photo interpretation error — that President Kennedy was reacting to a throat wound in Zapruder film frame No. 225 — put the Commission's investigators on the wrong track almost at the outset of their investigation.

The Single Bullet Theory

The Single Bullet Theory has no definition as such. It can best be described as a news title or caption used to identify certain logical straight-line deductions that could not be applied properly by the Commission's investigators — this because the logical deductions had been preempted by other erroneous deductions made earlier in their investigation.

In this particular instance, it can be said that the Commission's investigators generated a theory out of a set of circumstances (and evidence) that a properly conducted investigation readily proves to be factual.

It is being discussed here only because the circumstances that caused the Single Bullet Theory to emerge as such, epitomizes the whole series of investigative mistakes made by the President's Commission as it searched in vain for the solution to the mystery of the bullets.

As outlined in Chapter V, the Commission's investigators were called back, so to speak, by one of their own members to explain "some very persuasive evidence from the experts" which indicated that one bullet very probably had struck both President Kennedy and Governor Connally. It is interesting to note that this very persuasive evidence was medical and ballistic evidence that was, and still is, essentially irrefutable.

As best shown by the bullet combination chart, the Commission experienced no difficulty in accepting the possibility that a single bullet could have caused both the President's neck wound and Governor Connally's multiple wounds. The rub came when they tried to tie it in with the Zapruder pictures and Governor Connally's eyewitness account of when he was hit by this single bullet. When all this good evidence was put together, a very obvious inconsistency appeared. Although struck simultaneously by this single bullet, their reactions to having been struck appeared to occur almost one second apart, with the President reacting first.

This might be called the moment of decision for the Commisson's investigators but, unfortunately for them, they had already committed the investigative errors that would cause them to make the wrong choice which was to make no choice at all.

Their alternatives lay between reviewing their work to find an investigative mistake or oversight, and simply coming up with the assumption that Governor Connally had had a delayed reaction after having been struck and violently injured by a high-velocity rifle bullet. It must have been

108

right at this point that they recognized that they were on the "horns" of a dilemma — *and could make no choice at all.*

The more critical errors that put them in such a position can be categorized as follows:

1. The erroneous preconception that the first wound received by the President was his neck wound.

2. The photo interpretation error that established the second erroneous preconception that the President was reacting to having been struck in the neck when he came back into camera view from behind the road sign in film frame No. 225.

3 The use 'of irrelevant test data in establishing the rigid and controlling criterion that the bolt-action Mannlicher-Carcano rifle could not be fired at a rate faster than 2.3 seconds between shots with accuracy comparable with that demonstrated by the assassin.

4. The failure to establish investigative control by which they could rigidly control the input of evidence and testimony and thereby check and make the proper use of evidence available in the Zapruder film sequence and in the testimony of key eyewitnesses.

5. The failure to keep an open mind on the many bullet combinations and sequences possible when three bullets are fired at two men.

6. The general use of evaluative techniques and procedures in a case demanding straight-line investigative methods.

Suffice it to say in closing this chapter that the foregoing errors will not be made by us as we proceed to investigate into the assassination of President John F. Kennedy and the wounding of Governor John B. Connally, Jr.

Chapter VIII

INVESTIGATION AND SOLUTION

What is the scope of our investigation? We are going to determine how John Fitzgerald Kennedy, then President of the United States of America, was killed near high noon in Dealey Plaza, Dallas, Texas, on 22 November 1963.

By whom was he killed? This is beyond the scope of our investigation, except that certain qualifications and characteristics of the killer(s) will evolve as the investigation progresses.

> Author's Comment: All data, material evidence, and testimony used in our investigation is to be found in the official Report or in its supporting documentation. The author's continuing comments and remarks as he supervises this investigation will have to be accepted on the bases established in Parts I and II of this book or on their investigative merit.

111

Following a preliminary investigation, we will have acquired a considerable amount of general material evidence and testimony pointing up the *modus operandi* of the assassin(s) and the lethal instrument(s) used.

We have wounds caused by high-velocity bullets, the President with a visible neck and head wound, Governor Connally with a major wound in the back and less severe wounds in the wrist and thigh. By analyzing the wounds, we have the indication that the bullets inflicting these wounds were fired from an elevated position somewhere behind the line of travel of the presidential limousine. This line and direction of fire, when tied in with a whole bullet recovered from beneath Governor Connally's stretcher at Parkland Hospital, gives a strong indication that a bullet passed clean through the President's neck and continued on its line of flight to inflict all of Governor Connally's wounds, ending up spent in his clothing.

As material evidence, we have a high powered rifle, three expended cartridge cases from it, and one unexpended cartridge found in the chamber of the rifle — all found in the vicinity of a sixth-floor window of the Texas School Book Depository, an elevated position behind and looking almost directly down the line of travel taken by the presidential limousine as it rolled down the Elm Street straightaway.

The recovered whole bullet and several large bullet fragments found in the front compartment of the presidential limousine can be shown (ballistically) to have been fired from this rifle. A small star-crack on the interior surface of the limousine windshield and a dent in its upper chrome border give evidence of having been struck by hard objects coming from the direction of the rear of the limousine. The recovered bullet and the unexpended cartridge prove to be blunt-nosed full metal-jacketed bullets, and the two large fragments can be identified as a front and rear

112

(nose and base) section of the same type as the whole bullets.

We have various estimates from numerous accounts as to the number of loud and explosive noises or reports occurring while the presidential limousine traveled down Elm Street from the Depository to the Triple Underpass. The consensus among eyewitnesses directly on, or close to, the line of fire was that three loud, sharp, explosive reports occurred. The three expended cartridge cases found at the sixth-floor window of the Depository tend to substantiate this consensus.

We, like the President's Commission, have no credible material evidence that bullets were fired from any other point than from the sixth-floor window of the Texas School Book Depository.

We have eyewitness testimony in abundance. In fact, there are as many eyewitness accounts available to our investigating team as there were persons in or near Dealey Plaza at the time the President was assassinated. It is this over-abundance of testimony and volunteered opinions, among other good reasons, that requires us to immediately establish INVESTIGATIVE CONTROL by availing ourselves of a method, a mechanism, a measuring device that will permit us to identify and sift out the vital facts and happenings from the honest but ever fallible memories of a good many persons who were on the scene during the assassination.

Investigative Control

What is available to us in the way of a measuring stick? We need a common denominator, a sequence of factual reference points that can be identified or established and used to pin down the key episodes or critical moments in this tragic chain of events.

In the case at hand, we have the answer to an investigator's fondest wish — a continuous moving picture sequence with the presidential limousine in the center of its pictorial background from the time the limousine turned onto Elm Street until it went into the Triple Underpass leaving the scene of the assassination.

This 16-m/m film strip of consecutively numbered individual picture frames will have several exceedingly important applications in establishing investigative control.

> Author's Note: Reference will be made to specific Zapruder film frames (individual pictures) throughout our investigation. Individual frames will be identified by "Z" for Zapruder, followed by the serialized number given to each picture frame by the FBI (also used by *Life Magazine*) during the formal investigation.
>
> Word descriptions will be added where necessary for clarity, e.g., (Z-225, President coming back into view from behind road sign).

We are aware that the uniform cyclic operation of a moving picture camera permits us to accurately measure and determine time lapse, spatial position, rate and sequence of action, and the visual appearance and apparent action of all things photographed by the camera. With such a measuring device, reference or control points can be established easily almost anywhere along the route of travel of the presidential limousine as it ran the assassin's gantlet down the Elm Street straightaway.

For example, it can be accurately determined that the presidential limousine averaged 11.2 mph of speed down the 100 feet of Elm Street which it traveled while under the assassin(s) fire. But of even greater importance to the investigator is the use of the Zapruder film sequence in checking, correlating and cross-referencing testimony and other material evidence where time lapse, position, or sequence of action is critical. The use of the film strip in checking eye-witness accounts and other material evidence in these respects is similar to the check used to identify persons by their fingerprints or the ballistics checks made to determine that bullets were fired from a certain gun.

Eyewitness accounts are checked or correlated with mathematically calculated control or reference points. As an example, an eyewitness standing on the Grassy Knoll just abeam of the *calculated* road position of the presidential limousine where Z-313 shows visible matter first *appearing* out of the top of the President's head, testifies that he heard the last of a series of three loud reports and simultaneously saw the top of the President's head blow off. The testimony of this eyewitness and our control point Z-313 concide. This tells us as investigators that his testimony is very accurate as to time and place and is in the correct sequence of action as correlated with other control points. This eyewitness' testimony would become strong corroborative evidence in support of a tentative conclusion that President Kennedy was struck in the head at this road position by a bullet that caused the massive head wound found in the autopsy.

Another witness standing near the same place on the Grassy Knoll testifies that the presidential limousine was traveling so fast, 25 to 30 miles per hour in his opinion, and things happened so fast that he became very excited and did not see anything happen to the President, but he did think he heard seven shots. Our control here is having the calculated 11.2 mph average speed of the presidential limousine and strong indications that only three bullets were fired. A trained investigator would disregard this witness' testimony in its entirety.

Another valuable use of our control or reference points is in adjusting good testimony to known positions in the chain or sequence of events. A witness states that he clearly remembers that (an incident) occurred at (point A). A Z-frame clearly and positively establishes that the incident occurred at (point B). This testimony may be accepted on its merit but it would be adjusted to (point B) if used in evidence.

Selection of Reference or Control Points

A review of the entire Zapruder film sequence will show three Z-frames in which unusual things *appeared to occur* to the main actors in this tragic real-life drama. These will become three of our principal control points. A road position determined by engineering survey will furnish us with a fourth Z-frame control point. Our fifth control point will be a designated road position.

Station "C" — the point of intersection of the west curb line of Houston Street with the centerline of Elm Street. The point at which the motorcade turned off Houston Street onto Elm Street.

Control point Z-206 — the earliest point (approximately 135 feet down Elm Street from Station "C") at which a rifleman would have the first unobstructed telescopic sighting on the President from the eastern-most sixth-floor window of the Texas School Book Depository, as the presidential limousine moves down the Elm Street straightaway.

Control point Z-225 — the point at which President Kennedy comes back into camera view in the Zapruder film sequence after having been blocked from sight for approximately one second of time by an intervening road sign. At this point, President Kennedy *appears* to be reacting to having been struck.

116

Control point Z-236 — the point at which Governor Connally first *appears* to be reacting to having been struck.

Control point Z-313 — the point at which visible matter *appears* to burst out of President Kennedy's head.

Two additional investigator's tools will be required.

1. A Map-plan layout of the general area in which the assassination took place showing Station "C" and the road locations of the four Z-frame control points. See Map-plan, page 118.

2. A line and angle chart showing the relationship of Station "C" and the four Z-frame control points to elapsed time, road distance — and to the rifleman's position in the sixth-floor window of the Texas School Book Depository. See Chart, page 119.

We Call Witnesses

The eyewitness accounts that follow are a matter of public record, in question and answer form, in the testimony taken by the President's Commission. The official testimony that follows is recorded verbatim in a Bantam Book publication titled, *The Witnesses,* published in December 1964. For those desiring such reference, the symbol (Wit-pp.——) will be used to identify the pages where the testimony appears in that publication.

References to Zapruder camera pictures (Z-frames) will be interjected into the testimony as annotations at points where a condition or a road position identifies itself with a particular Z-frame. If the Z-frame coincides with one of our

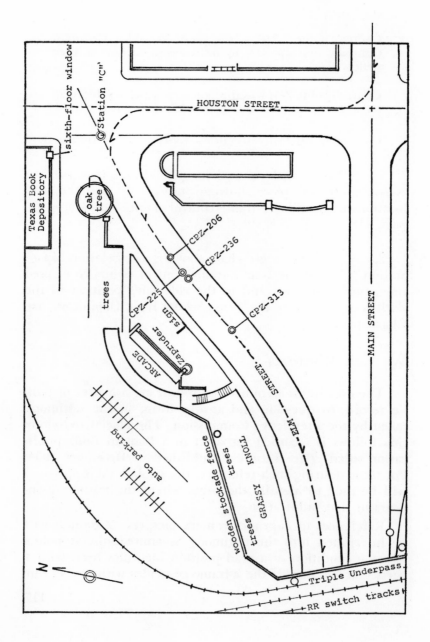

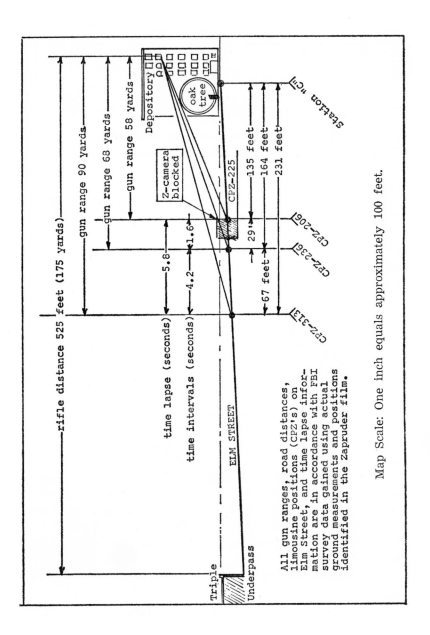

Map Scale: One inch equals approximately 100 feet.

rifle distance 525 feet (175 yards)

gun range 90 yards

gun range 68 yards

gun range 58 yards

Depository

oak tree

Z-camera blocked

CPZ-225

135 feet

164 feet

231 feet

Station "C"

CPZ-206

CPZ-236

CPZ-313

29'

67 feet

5.8

1.6

4.2

time lapse (seconds)

time intervals (seconds)

ELM STREET

Triple

Underpass

All gun ranges, road distances,
limousine positions (CPZ's) on
Elm Street, and time lapse information are in accordance with FBI
survey data gained using actual
ground measurements and positions
identified in the Zapruder film.

control points, it will be preceded by (CP), e.g., Governor Connally testifies, "I felt like something had hit me in the back (CPZ-236)."

Testimony of Governor John B. Connally, Jr., who was seated in the right jump seat of the presidential limousine immediately in front of President Kennedy.

(Wit-pp. 19-23)

Mr. Specter. (Warren Commission interrogator) As the automobile turned left onto Elm from Houston (Station "C"), what did occur there, Governor?

A — We had — we had gone, I guess, 150 feet (near CPZ-206) maybe 200 feet, I don't recall how far it was, heading down to get on the freeway, the Stemmons Freeway, to go out to the Hall where we were going to have lunch and, as I say, the crowds had begun to thin, and we could — I was anticipating that we were going to be at the Hall in approximately 5 minutes from the time we turned on Elm Street.

We had just made the turn, well, when I heard what I thought was a shot (near CPZ-206 as above). I heard this noise which I immediately took to be a rifle shot. I instinctively turned to my right because the sound appeared to come from over my right shoulder, so I turned to look back over my right shoulder (before CPZ-225) and saw nothing unusual except just the people in the crowd but I did not catch the President in the corner of my eye, and I was interested, because once I heard the shot in my own mind I identified it as a rifle shot, and I immediately — the only thought that crossed my mind was that this is an assassination attempt.

So I looked, failing to see him, I was turning (CPZ-225)

120

to look back over my left shoulder into the back seat, but I never got that far in my turn. I got about in the position I am in now facing you, looking a little bit to the left of center, and then I felt like someone had hit me in the back (CPZ-236).

Mr. Specter. What is the best estimate that you have as to the time span between the sound of the first shot and the feeling of someone hitting you in the back which you just described? (Z-206 to Z-236 measures 1.6 seconds.)

A — A very, very brief span of time. Again my trend of thought just happened to be, I suppose along this line, I immediately thought that this — that I had been shot. I knew it when I just looked down and I was covered with blood, and the thought immediately passed through my mind that there were either two or three people involved or more in this or someone was shooting with an automatic rifle. These were just thoughts that went through my mind because of the rapidity of these two, of the first shot plus the blow that I took, and I knew I had been hit, and I immediately assumed, because of the amount of blood, and, in fact, that it had obviously passed through my chest, that I had probably been fatally hit.

So I merely doubled up, and then turned to my right again and began to — I just sat there, and Mrs. Connally pulled me over to her lap. She was sitting, of course, on the jump seat, so I reclined with my head in her lap, conscious all the time, and with my eyes open; and then, of course, the third shot sounded (CPZ-313), and I heard the shot very clearly. I heard it hit him. I heard the shot hit something, and I assumed again — it never entered my mind that it ever hit anybody but the President. I heard it hit. It was a very loud noise, just that audible, very clear.

Immediately I could see on my clothes, my clothing, I could see on the interior of the car which, as I recall, was

121

a pale blue, brain tissue, which I immediately recognized (all after Z-313), and I recall very well, on my trousers there was one chunk of brain tissue as big as almost my thumb, thumbnail, and again I did not see the President at any time either after the first (about CPZ-206), second (CPZ-236), or third shots (CPZ-313), but I assumed always that it was he who was hit and no one else.

I immediately, when I was hit, I said, "Oh, no, no, no." (after CPZ-236) and then I said, "My God, they are going to kill us all." Nellie, when she pulled me over into her lap —

Mr. Specter. Nellie is Mrs. Connally?

A — Mrs. Connally. When she pulled me over into her lap, she could tell I was still breathing and moving, and she said, "Don't worry. Be quiet. You are going to be all right." She just kept telling me I was going to be all right.

After the third shot (CPZ-313), and I heard Roy Kellerman tell the driver, "Bill, get out of line." And then I saw him move, and I assumed he was moving a button or something on the panel of the automobile, and he said, "Get us to a hospital quick." I assumed he was saying this to the patrolman, the motorcycle police who were leading us.

At about that time (well past CPZ-313), we began to pull out of the cavalcade, out of line, and I lost consciousness and didn't regain consciousness until we got to the hospital. . . .

Mr. Specter. Governor, you have described hearing a first shot and a third shot. Did you hear a second shot?

A — No; I did not.

Mr. Specter. What is your best estimate as to the time-span between the first shot which you heard and the shot which you heretofore characterized as the third shot? (Z-206 to Z-313 measures 5.8 seconds.)

A — It was a very brief span of time; oh, I would have to say a matter of seconds. I don't know, 10, 12 seconds. It was extremely rapid, so much so that again I thought that whoever was firing must be firing with an automatic rifle because of the rapidity of the shots; a very short period of time.

Mr. Specter. What was your impression then as to the source of the shot?

A — From back over my right shoulder which, again, was where immediately when I heard the first shot I identified the sound as coming back over my right shoulder.

Mr. Specter. At an elevation?

A — At an elevation. I would have guessed at an elevation.

Mr. Specter. Excuse me.

A — Well, that is all.

Mr. Specter. Did you have an impression as to the source of the third shot?

A — The same. I would say the same. . . .

Mr. Specter. Did President Kennedy make any statement during the time of the shooting or immediately prior thereto?

A — He never uttered a sound at all that I heard.

Mr. Specter. Did Mrs. Kennedy state anything at that time?

A — Yes; I have to — I would say it was after the third shot when she said, "They have killed my husband."

Mr. Specter. Did she say anything more?

A — Yes; she said, I heard her say one time, "I have got his brains in my hand."

Mr. Specter. Did that constitute everything that she said at the time?

A — That is all I heard her say.

Mr. Specter. Did Mrs. Connally say anything further at this time?

A — All she said to me was, after I was hit when she

123

pulled me over in her lap, she said, "Be quiet, you are going to be all right. Be still, you are going to be all right." She just kept repeating that. . . .

Mr. Specter. Did you observe any reaction by President Kennedy after the shooting?

A — No; I did not see him.

Mr. Specter. Did you observe any reaction by Mrs. Kennedy after the shooting?

A — I did not see her. This almost sounds incredible, I am sure, since we were in the car with them. But again I will repeat very briefly when what I believe to be the first shot occurred (CPZ-206 — Z-215), I turned to my right, which was away from both of them, of course, and looked out (Z-215 — CPZ-225) and could see neither, and then as I was turning to look into the back seat (CPZ-225) where I would have seen both of them, I was hit (CPZ-236), so I never completed the turn at all, and I never saw either one of them after the firing started, and, of course, as I have testified, then Mrs. Connaly pulled me over into her lap and I was facing forward with my head slightly turned up to where I could see the driver and Roy Kellerman on his right, but I could not see into the back seat, so I didn't see either one of them.

Mr. Specter. When you turned to your right, Governor Connally, immediately after you heard the first shot, what did you see on that occasion?

A — Nothing of any significance except just people out on the grass slope. I didn't see anything that was out of the ordinary, just saw men, women, and children.

Mr. Specter. Do you have any estimate as to the distance which the President's automobile traveled during the shooting? (Z-206 to Z-313 measures 96 feet.)

A — No; I hadn't thought about it, but I would suppose

124

in 10 to 12 seconds (Z-206 to Z-313 measures 5.8 seconds), I suppose you travel a couple of hundred feet.

Mr. Specter. Did you observe any bullet or fragments of bullet strike the metal chrome?

A — No.

Mr. Specter. Did you experience any sensation of being struck any place other than that which you have described on your chest?

A — No.

Mr. Specter. What other wounds, if any, did you sustain?

A — A fractured wrist and a wound in the thigh, just above the knee.

Mr. Specter. What thigh?

A — Left thigh; just above the knee.

Mr. Specter. Where on the wrist were you injured, sir?

A — I don't know how you describe it.

Mr. Specter. About how many inches up from the wrist joint?

A — I would say an inch above the wrist bone, but on the inner bone of the wrist where the bullet went in here and came out almost in the center of the wrist on the underside.

Mr. Specter. About an inch from the base of the palm?

A — About an inch from the base of the palm, a little less than an inch, three-quarters of an inch.

Mr. Specter. Were you conscious of receiving that wound on the wrist at the time you sustained it?

A — No sir; I was not.

Mr. Specter. When did you first know you were wounded in the right wrist?

A — When I came to in the hospital on Saturday, the next morning, and I looked up and my arm was tied up in a hospital bed, and I said, "What is wrong with my

125

arm?" And they told me then that I had a shattered wrist, and that is when I also found out I had a wound in the thigh.

Mr. Specter. Can you describe the nature of the wound in the thigh?

A — Well, just a raw, open wound, looked like a fairly deep penetration.

Mr. Specter. Indicating about 2 inches?

A — No; I would say about an inch, an inch and a quarter long is all; fairly wide, I would say a quarter of an inch wide, maybe more, a third of an inch wide, and about an inch and a quarter, an inch and a half long.

Mr. Specter. Were you conscious that you had been wounded on the left thigh at the time it occurred?

A — No.

Mr. Specter. Did you first notice that in the hospital on the following day also?

A — Yes.

Mr. Specter. In your view, which bullet caused the injury to your chest, Governor Connally?

A — The second one (CPZ-236).

Mr. Specter. And what is your reason for that conclusion, sir?

A — Well, in my judgment, it just couldn't conceivably have been the first one (CPZ-206 — Z-215) because I heard the sound of the shot. In the first place, I don't know anything about the velocity of this particular bullet, but any rifle has a velocity that exceeds the speed of sound, and when I heard the sound of that first shot, that bullet had already reached where I was, or it had reached that far, and after I heard that shot, I had the time to turn to my right, and start to turn to my left before I felt anything.

It is not conceivable to me that I could have been hit

126

by the first bullet, and then I felt the blow from something which was obviously a bullet, which I assumed was a bullet, and I never heard the second shot, didn't hear it. I didn't hear but two shots. I think I heard the first shot and the third shot.

Mr. Specter. Do you have any idea as to why you did not hear the second shot?

A — Well, first, again I assume the bullet was traveling faster than sound. I was hit by the bullet prior to the time the sound reached me, and I was either in a state of shock or the impact was such that the sound didn't register on me, but I was never conscious of hearing the second shot at all. Obviously, at least the major wound that I took in the shoulder through the chest couldn't have been anything but the second shot. Obviously, it couldn't have have been the third, because when the third shot was fired I was in a reclining position, and heard it, saw it and the effects of it, rather — I didn't see it, I saw the effects of it — so it obviously could not have been the third, and couldn't have been the first, in my judgment.

Mr. Specter. What was the nature of the exit wound on the front side of your chest, Governor?

Note: Doctors Shaw and Gregory, who had treated Governor Connally's wounds, were present during the interrogation. Using the Governor's person to demonstrate, they gave the following expert testimony to the Commission on the nature of the wounds received by Governor Connally.

·　·　·　·　·

(Wit-pp. 24-31)

Mr. Specter. Will you describe the location, Doctor, of that wound on the Governor's back?

Dr. Shaw. Yes. It is on the right shoulder, I will mete

127

it just lateral to the shoulder blade, the edge of which is about 2 centimeters from the wound, and just above and slightly medial to the crease formed by the axilla or the armpit, the arm against the chest wall.

` > , • • •

Mr. Specter. Will you now, Doctor, describe the location of the wound of exit on the Governor's chest please?

Dr. Shaw. Yes. The wound of exit was beneath and medial to the nipple. Here was this V that I was indicating. It is almost opposite that. At the time of the wound there was a ragged oval hole here at least 5 centimeters in diameter (about 2 inches) but the skin edges were excised, and here again this scar . . .

• • • • •

Senator Cooper. (Member of the Commission) I am just trying to remember whether we asked you, Doctor, if you probed the wound in the thigh to see how deep it was?

Dr. Gregory. I did not, Senator. Dr. Tom Shires at our institution attended that wound, and I have his description to go on, what he found, what he had written, and his description is that it did not penetrate the thigh very deeply, just to the muscle, but not beyond that.

Representative Boggs. (Member of the Commission) Just one other question of the Doctor. Having looked at the wound, there is no doubt in either of your minds that the bullet came from the rear, is there?

Dr. Gregory. There has never been any doubt in my mind about the origin of the missile; no.

Representative Boggs. And in yours?

Dr. Shaw. No.

. . . . .

(Wit-pp. 32-34)

Mr. Specter. Governor Connally, other than that which you have already testified to, do you know of any events or occurrences either before the trip or with the President in Texas during his trip, or after his trip, which could shed any light on the assassination itself?

A — None whatever.

Mr. Specter. Do you have anything to add which you think would be helpful to the Commission in any way?

A — No, sir; Mr. Specter, I don't.

I want to express my gratitude to the Commission for hearing me so patiently, but I only wish I could have added something more that would be helpful to the Commission on arriving at the many answers to so many of these difficult problems, but I don't.

I can only say that it has taken some little time to describe the events and what happened. It is rather amazing in retrospect when you think really what a short period of time it took for it to occur, in a matter of seconds (about 5.8 seconds), and if my memory is somewhat vague about precisely which way I was looking or where my hand or arm was, I can only say I hope it is understandable in the light of the fact that this was a very sudden thing. It was a very shocking thing.

I have often wondered myself why I never had the presence of mind enough — I obviously did say something I said, "Oh, no, no, no," and then I said, "My God, they are going to kill us all."

I don't know why I didn't say, "Get down in the car," but I didn't. You just never know why you react the way you do and why you don't do some things you ought to do.

But I am again grateful to this Commission as a participant in this tragedy and as a citizen of this country, and I want to express, I think in behalf of millions of people, our gratitude for the time and energy and the dedication that this Commission has devoted to trying to supply the answers that people, I am sure, will be discussing for generations to come. I know it has been a difficult, long, laborious task for you, but I know that generations of the future Americans will be grateful for your efforts.

Representative Boggs. Governor, I would like to say that we have had fine cooperation from all of your Texas officials, from the attorney general of the State, and from his people and others who have worked with the Commission.

A — Well, we are delighted, and I am very happy that the attorney general is here with us today.

Senator Cooper. May I ask one question?

The Chairman. Yes, Senator Cooper.

Senator Cooper. Governor, at the time you all passed the Texas School Book Depository, did you know that such a building was located there? Were you familiar with the building at all?

A — Just vaguely, Senator.

Senator Cooper. But now when you heard the shot, you turned to your right because you thought, as you said, that the shot came from that direction. As you turned, was that in the direction of the Texas School Book Depository?

A — Yes, sir; it was.

Senator Cooper. Do you remember an overpass in front of you —

A — Yes, sir.

Senator Cooper. As you moved down?

A — Yes, sir.

130

Senator Cooper. Were you aware at all of any sounds of rifle shots from the direction of the overpass, from the embankment?

A — No, sir; I don't believe there were such.

Senator Cooper. Well, you know, there have been stories.

A — Yes, sir; but I don't believe that.

Senator Cooper. I want to ask you if you were very conscious of the fact — you were conscious of a shot behind you, you were not aware of any shot from the embankment or overpass. The answer is what?

A — I am not aware of any shots from the overpass, Senator. Senator, I might repeat my testimony with emphasis to this extent, that I have all my life been familiar with the sound of a rifleshot, and that sound I heard I thought was a rifleshot, at the time I heard it I didn't think it was a firecracker or blowout or .anything else. I thought it was a rifleshot. I have hunted enough to think that my perception with respect to directions is very, very good, and this shot I heard came from back over my right shoulder, which was in the direction of the School Book Depository, no question about it. I heard no other. The first (CPZ-206) and third (CPZ-313) shots came from there. I heard no other sounds that would indicate to me there was any commotion or disturbance of shots or anything else on the overpass.

Senator Cooper. Would you describe again the nature of the shock you had when you felt that you had been hit by a bullet?

A — Senator, the best way I can describe it is to say that I would say it is as if someone doubled his fist and came up behind you and just with about a 12-inch blow hit you right in the back right below the shoulder blade.

Senator Cooper. That is when you heard the first rifleshot?

131

A — This was after I heard the first rifleshot. There was no pain connected with it. There was no particular burning sensation. There was nothing more than that. I think you would feel almost the identical sensation I felt if someone came up behind you and just, with a short jab, hit you with a doubled-up fist just below the shoulder blade. . . .

Mr. Dulles. I have one or two . . .

(End of testimony pertinent to our line of investigation)

Governor Connally's testimony parallels our investigative control schedule as follows:

Control point	Elapsed time (seconds)	Governor Connally's key testimony.
CPZ-206	Zero	. . . . . Hears first rifle report.
CPZ-225	1.0 sec.	Turns to right and then immediately back towards left.
CPZ-236	1.6 sec.	Struck in back (hears no rifle report) Utters, "Oh, no, no, no." Utters, "My God, they are going to kill us all."
CPZ-313	5.8 sec.	Hears shot sound — hears something get hit in limousine. Hit in limousine was "a very loud noise, just that audible, very clear." Sees animal matter fall on clothing and on limousine. Lapses into unconsciousness.

Investigative analysis and check of Governor Connally's eyewitness account.

The analysis of any testimony starts with a qualification of the witness giving the testimony. Experienced investigators estimate the general alertness and perceptiveness of a witness and his degree of expertness in technical or specialized aspects of the circumstances under investigation.

An experienced *interrogator* makes it a point to determine the overall expertness of the witness — during the interrogation. This is often done by direct questioning. It is to be noted that Governor Connally volunteered this information as regards his long experience as a hunter and his familiarity with high powered rifles — when the Commission's interrogators failed to solicit it.

Our first check of the eyewitness account or story itself is for overall plausibility, continuity, and whether or not it lies in the realm of possibility considering known and measurable technical and physical phenomena. This, then, is considered in relation to our overall qualification of the witness.

In the light of the foregoing, we find Governor Connally's testimony to be plausible and well within the realm of technical possibility. We note that Governor Connally is an alert and perceptive individual; an experienced and knowledgeable witness. His testimony is straightforward, near-expert as regards high powered rifles, and it has unbroken continuity through the circumstances under investigation.

Our investigative control shows us that Governor Connally's testimony matches very closely with two of our control points, CPZ-236 and CPZ-313.

According to his testimony, his actions on hearing a rifle report from back over his right shoulder were to turn

133

around to the right and then immediately start a turn back to the left, being struck just after his turn to the left had brought him back to facing front again. A check of Z-frames Z-222 (Governor Connally first comes back into view from behind road sign) through our CPZ-225 and on to our CPZ-236 shows Governor Connally doing exactly this.

He testifies that he was struck in the back as he passed through facing front in his turn to the left. Our CPZ-236 shows Governor Connally appearing to initiate a reaction to having been struck — he is facing front and previous Z-frames show that he was turning from right to left. His testimony and CPZ-236 coincide.

He testifies that after having been struck, and after a very brief interval of time during which he was fully conscious, he heard another rifle report sound from the same direction as the initial rifle report, that he heard something get hit in the limousine, and that he simultaneously saw what he took to be human tissue or brain matter fall out of the air onto himself and onto the surfaces of the limousine. Our CPZ-313 shows Governor Connally to be in the position that he testified to having been in (reclining against Mrs. Connally) at the time he heard a final rifle report. Z-313 also shows visible matter appearing to emanate rapidly (it is not visible 1/20 of a second before in Z-312) from the President's head. Our CPZ-313 and Governor Connally's testimony are in sequential alignment, coincide within nominal limits, and both are corroborative in support of a tentative deduction that President Kennedy received a head wound (with its massive consequence) at CPZ-313.

Governor Connally's testimony has the sequence of these critical happenings in the correct order according to our control points. He estimates a very brief span of time

134

between the initial and final rifle report that he heard. His testimony indicates that the time interval between the initial rifle report and his being struck was somewhat briefer than the time interval between his being struck and his hearing the final rifle report. These are all in consonance with data calculated from the Zapruder film sequence.

Several vital pieces of information need tying down in point of time or position.

According to his testimony, the presidential limousine had turned onto Elm Street and had proceeded 150 to 200 feet (his rough estimate) down Elm Street when he heard the initial rifle report. Our CPZ-206, the earliest point affording unobstructed telescopic sighting from the sixth-floor window of the Depository, measures about 135 feet down Elm Street from our Station "C," the point at which the presidential limousine turned onto Elm Street from Houston Street. Governor Connally testifies that on hearing the first rifle report, he turned to the right and immediately back toward the left, a maneuver that would take the better part of a second. Our CPZ-225 is a point only 19 feet and one second of time farther down Elm Street than our CPZ-206, but at CPZ-225 we see him turning back to the left after his having (as he testified) turned first to the right. It is a reasonable deduction that he heard the first shot the better part of a second before our CPZ-225 which puts the initial rifle report very near our CPZ-206.

His testimony, "I immediately, when I was hit, I said, 'Oh, no, no, no,' and then I said, 'My God, they are going to kill us all,' " needs better correlation with his hearing the initial rifle report and his realizing that he had been struck. The timing of the start of his ejaculation, "Oh, no, no, no," is critical (although not vital) to our

135

investigation so we will take every investigative step possible to tie it down in point of time.

His testimony would indicate that he uttered both expressions, with the ejaculation first, after he had been struck at CPZ-236. We see that he was not cross-examined or made to specify on this point during his interrogation. In reviewing his testimony, we find the following statement made by Governor Connally to the Commission as a closing remark near the end of his formal interrogation.

. . . . . .

A — I can only say that it has taken some little time to describe the events and what happened. It is rather amazing in retrospect when you think really what a short period of time it took for it to occur, in a matter of seconds, *and if my memory is somewhat vague about precisely which way I was looking or where my hand or arm was,* I can only say I hope it is understandable in the light of the fact that this was a very sudden thing. It was a very shocking thing.

. . . . . .

Our experience as trained investigators tells us that utterances which are a part of the *res gestae* are least remembered by the persons who made them — and this by reason of the overriding shock that calls them forth.

We are also aware that utterances which are a part of the *res gestae* usually come into evidence as hearsay and are admissible because such utterances are better and more clearly remembered by those who hear them rather than by those who utter them. We have two witnesses who will testify that Governor Connally started to utter, "Oh! no, no," after the initial rifle report — but before he was struck at CPZ-236.

136

Considering Governor Connally's responsibilities at that moment and his attendant alertness, it would be extremely improbable that he would have heard and instantly recognized a rifle report as an assassination attempt and simultaneously turned to the right trying to locate its source — without uttering an ejaculation of some sort.

Except for the start of his initial ejaculation, Governor Connally's testimony has checked out against all of our control points and, for the purposes of our investigation to this point, can be considered a very credible account of what took place within his purview.

Considering all evidence and testimony available to us at this point in our investigation, we make the following tentative deductions:

1. A rifle report occurred when the presidential limousine was at or near the road position designated as our CPZ-206.

2. Governor Connally was struck in the back by a bullet fired from an elevated position rearward of the presidential limousine, at or very near the road position designated as our CPZ-236.

3. A rifle report occurred when the presidential limousine was at or near the road position designated as our CPZ-313. At this same point, President Kennedy was struck in the back of the head by a bullet fired from a position rearward of the presidential limousine. A massive exit wound in the top of the President's head resulted from this bullet.

We have raised and we carry forward an investigative question: "Was Governor Connally's ejaculation, 'Oh, no, no, no,' uttered as a result of his hearing the initial rifle report or was it uttered as a result of his having been struck in the back?"

We call our next witness.

Silent testimony of John Fitzgerald Kennedy, President of the United States of America. The President was seated on the right side of the rear seat of the presidential limousine.

Using Station "C" and our four control points, we can make certain determinations with regard to President Kennedy as he appears in the Zapruder film sequence. From Station "C" (his turning onto Elm Street) until CPZ-206 (first unobstructed rifle sighting), the President, with his head held high and turned toward the right, was waving to the people on his right with his elevated right arm.

From about four Z-frames ahead of CPZ-206 until our CPZ-225 (1.2 seconds of time), the President was not in Zapruder camera view due to an intervening road sign. As he came into view again at CPZ-225, *he appeared to be reacting to having been struck!*

> Author's Comment: Undoubtedly, this is the point, literally and geographically, at which the Commission made its first serious investigative mistake. The President's autopsy had disclosed only two points at which bullets had entered his body, the back of his head and his back at the base of the neck. All evidence indicated that the head wound was the final wound inflicted. Therefore, reasoned the Commission, the President *must be* reacting to the other wound, the neck wound, when he reappears from behind the road sign at CPZ-225. We shall see that this reasoning was both faulty and misleading.

138

As President Kennedy comes back into view from behind the road sign, CPZ-225, he is seen to have his head erect, if not tilted back slightly, chin up, and facing about half right. It is interesting to note that at this instant (Z-225), President Kennedy is facing directly toward or into the Zapruder camera. His mouth appears to be open as though he is voicing something and his eyes appear to be batted shut. His facial expression could be called dazed or stunned. His elbows are down somewhat below shoulder level and his hands are one over the other at breast-bone level. *He appears to be reacting to having been struck.*

In the brief instant of time between CPZ-225 and CPZ-236 (measured at 0.6 of a second), the President is seen to duck (hunch) forward and slightly to his left while rapidly throwing his elbows upward and forward to about ear level. Simultaneously, his hands move up and out in front of his face to chin level.

The President definitely *is not* grasping at his throat. His entire reaction from somewhere before Z-225 until about Z-236 is a characteristic *reflexive* reaction to a sharp blow on the head when struck unexpectedly from the rear.

His ducking or hunching action, which amounts to pulling the shoulder blades up and over the spine at the base of the neck, is a semi-voluntary reaction, occurring at reflex speeds, in anticipation of a second sharp blow on the head — following on the first.

The physical (autopsy) evidence showed that the point of entry of the bullet causing the President's neck wound was in the neck-shoulder saddle, 5½ inches below the right mastoid process, the bony point immediately behind the ear, and 5½ inches inward from the tip of the right shoulder joint. The exit point (the bullet passed clean through) was located in the lower third of the neck (in front) below the Adam's apple.

President Kennedy's suit jacket displayed a bullet hole in the back, $5\frac{3}{8}$ inches below the top of the collar and $1\frac{3}{4}$ inches to the right of the center back seam of the coat. His shirt had a hole in the back $5\frac{3}{4}$ inches below the top of the collar and $1\frac{1}{8}$ inches to the right of the middle of the back of the shirt. On the front of the shirt, there was a hole $\frac{7}{8}$ of an inch below the collar button hole, and a nick in the knot of the tie.

Our investigation thus far has determined that from the turn onto Elm Street to a little before CPZ-225, the President was sitting upright and was looking at and waving to people on his right.

Assuming (for test purposes only) that the neck wound was received before our CPZ-225 while the President was sitting upright with his right arm elevated, and the shot was fired from the elevated sixth-floor window of the Depository at a 20-degree angle downward, it is a logical deduction that the bullet would pass through the President's body on a downward course with relation to his upright body position and would continue on its downward course (relative to the horizontal) to strike Governor Connally below his right armpit — but physical (autopsy) evidence shows the reverse to be true.

As the critics were quick to notice, a bullet entering the back at a point $5\frac{3}{4}$ inches below the top of the shirt collar, and coming out at the collar button in the front — if the person was sitting bolt upright with head held high — would be moving on a horizontal or slightly rising course rather than on a downward course.

Author's Comment: This investigative bias is typical

of the many "misfits" between testimony and material evidence that occurred when the Commission tried to tie or pull together the two wounds of the Single Bullet Theory with their preconception that the first bullet had caused the President's neck wound. The widest misfit growing out of this, of course, was Governor Connally's *seemingly delayed* physical reaction to having been struck in the back — by this *early* bullet.

The tragedy of all this erroneous reasoning was that it led the Commission to doubt Governor Connally's testimony — the very accuracy of which lays the foundation upon which the solution to this mystery is built.

The logical investigator's question growing out of the *seemingly rising* path of the bullet is, "What position did the President have to be in to cause a bullet, fired downward from an elevated position to his rear, to take this seemingly rising course through the base of his neck?" The reasoning is elemental — he had to be ducking (hunching) forward with his shoulder blades pulled up (protectively) over the base of the back of his neck.

The reader's attention is directed to CPZ-236, the point at which (a) Governor Connally testifies that he received his back wound, (b) our CPZ-236 shows Governor Connally *appearing* to react to just having been struck, (c) President Kennedy is seen to be ducking (hunching) his shoulders in position to receive a *seemingly rising* neck wound, and (d) the alignment of the President and Governor Connally to the line of the "single bullet" is seen to be exactly as it would have to be for one bullet (the second bullet fired) to strike both men.

If the Zapruder picture series is at hand (25 Nov. 1966 issue of *Life Magazine*), note very carefully the President's

141

shoulder, head, and hand positions in Z-236, and then note the secondary reaction, the head turning slightly left and hands rising slightly and moving closer to the face, that takes place on up to Z-242. This, very likely, is all the ballistic impact reaction that would result from a full-jacketed bullet passing cleanly through the flesh of the right side of the President's neck — at near maximum velocity.

> Author's Comment: A reasonable question arises at this point. "Was this bullet deflected by its passage through the President's neck?"
>
> Passing as it did through the right side of the President's neck, its ballistic tendency, not striking bone, would be to deflect to the right away from the denser tissue of the neck and spine that would be to its left in passing.
>
> A survey of the lateral alignment of President Kennedy and Governor Connally at CPZ-236 with relation to the sixth-floor window of the Depository indicates that this single bullet would have had to deflect slightly to the right to have struck Governor Connally on his right side. The amount of deflection needed is well within the deflection possible under the ballistic circumstances and conditions that pertain. The fact that Governor Connally was struck near his *right armpit* simply turns a ballistic probability into a ballistic certainty.

President Kennedy's silent testimony parallels our investigative control schedule as follows:

Control point	Elapsed time	The President's silent testimony.
CPZ-206	Zero	President sitting erect and waving right arm to people on his right.
CPZ-225	1.0 sec.	*President in reaction to having been struck.*

142

CPZ-236 1.6 sec. President in ducking (hunching) position required to receive the *seemingly rising* neck wound.

CPZ-313 5.8 sec. Visible matter seen to burst from the top of the President's head.

Considering all evidence and testimony available to us at this point, we make the following tentative deductions.

1. A rifle shot occurred when the presidential limousine was at or very near the road position designated as our CPZ-206. *President Kennedy was struck by this shot.*

2. A second rifle shot occurred when the rear of the presidential limousine was at the road point designated as our CPZ-236. President Kennedy was struck by a bullet which passed clean through his neck and continued on to strike Governor Connally in the back, right wrist, and left thigh, in that order, ending up spent in Governor Connally's clothing. This bullet was fired from an elevated position in rear of the presidential limousine.

3. A third rifle shot occurred when the presidential limousine was at the road position designated as our CPZ-313. At this same point President Kennedy was struck in the back of the head by a bullet fired from a position rearward of the presidential limousine. A massive exit wound in the top of the President's head resulted from this bullet.

We carry forward the investigative question, "Was Governor Connally's ejaculation, 'Oh, no, no, no,' uttered as the result of his hearing the initial rifle report or was it uttered after he had been struck in the back by the second bullet?"

We ask another investigative question: "What is the evidence, if any, to indicate the possibility of the massive exit wound in the top of the President's head being a *multiple wound?"*

We call our next witness.

Testimony of Mrs. John B. Connally, Jr., wife of the Governor of Texas, who was seated in the left jump seat of the presidential limousine, immediately in front of Mrs. Kennedy.

(Wit-pp. 36-37)

Mr. Specter. (Warren Commission interrogator) Mrs. Connally, tell us what happened at the time of the assassination.

A — We had just finished the motorcade through the downtown Dallas area, and it had been a wonderful motorcade. The people had been very responsive to the President and Mrs. Kennedy, and we were very pleased, I was very pleased.

As we got off Main Street — is that the main thoroughfare?

Mr. Specter. That is the street on which you were proceeding through the town, yes.

A — In fact the receptions had been so good every place that I had showed much restraint by not mentioning something about it before.

I could resist no longer. When we got past this area I did turn to the President and said, "Mr. President, you can't say Dallas doesn't love you."

Then I don't know how soon, it seems to me it was

144

very soon, that I heard a noise, and not being an expert rifleman, I was not aware that it was a rifle. It was just a frightening noise, and it came from the right.

I turned over my right shoulder and looked back, and saw the President as he had both hands at his neck (at or immediately after our CPZ-225).

Mr. Specter. And you are indicating with your own hands, two hands crossing over gripping your own neck?

> Author's Comment: A leading question to be sure. Mr. Specter was an exponent of the Single Bullet Theory (correct as it was) which, unfortunately, caused him to lead his witnesses into confirming the misconception that President Kennedy was reacting to the neck wound as he came back into view at our CPZ-225. Mrs. Connally had been apprised of the President's neck wound and the possibility of one bullet having struck both men, before the interrogation.

A — Yes; and it seemed to me there was — he made no utterance, no cry. I saw no blood, no anything. It was just sort of nothing, the expression on his face, and he just sort of slumped down (between Z-225 and Z-236).

Then very soon there was a second shot that hit John (CPZ-236). As the first shot was hit *(the frightening noise)*, and I turned to look at the same time (about Z-225), I recall John saying, "Oh, no, no, no." (started before CPZ-236) Then there was a second shot, and it hit John (CPZ-236), and as he recoiled to the right, just crumpled like a wounded animal to the right, he said, "My God, they are going to kill us all." (started after CPZ-236)

I never again —

Mr. Dulles. (member of the Commission) To the right was into your arms more or less?

A — No, he turned away from me. I was pretending

that I was him. I never again looked in the back seat of the car after my husband was shot. (after CPZ-236) My concern was for him, and I remember that he turned to the right and then just slumped down into the seat, so that I reached over to pull him toward me. I was trying to get him down and me down. The jump seats were not very roomy, so that there were reports that he slid into the seat of the car, which he did not; that he fell over into my lap, which he did not.

I just pulled him over into my arms because it would have been impossible to get us really both down with me sitting and holding him. So that I looked out, I mean as he was in my arms, I put my head down over his head so that his head and my head were right together, and all I could see, too, were the people flashing by. I didn't look back any more.

The third shot that I heard I felt (CPZ-313), it felt like spent buckshot falling all over us, and then, of course, I too could see that it was the matter, brain tissue, or whatever, just human matter, all over the car and both of us. (after CPZ-313)

I thought John had been killed, and then there was some imperceptible movement, just some little something that let me know that there was still some life, and that is when I started saying to him, "It's all right. Be still."

Now, I did hear the Secret Service man say, "Pull out of the motorcade. Take us to the nearest hospital," and then we took out very rapidly to the hospital.

.   .   .   .   .   .

(Wit-pp. 37-38)

Mr. Specter. Did President Kennedy say anything at all after the shooting?

A — He did not say anything. Mrs. Kennedy said, the

first thing I recall her saying was, after the first shot, and I heard her say, "Jack, they have killed my husband," and then there was the second shot and then after the third shot she said, "They have killed my husband. I have his brains in my hands," and she repeated that several times, and that was all the conversation.

Author's Comment: The foregoing answer given by Mrs. Connally is exceedingly critical testimony. This "hearsay" testimony indicates that Mrs. Kennedy started her first utterance, "Jack, they have killed my husband," immediately after the first shot (CPZ-206) but before the second shot that hit Governor Connally at CPZ-236 which was the second shot according to Mrs. Connally. This utterance then becomes a part of the *res gestae* of the first shot as it affected Mrs. Kennedy on looking at the President immediately after the first shot was fired. The criticalness of the timing of this first utterance will be appreciated when we hear Mrs. Kennedy's testimony.

Mrs. Kennedy's second utterance, "They have killed my husband. I have his brains in my hands," was heard by Mrs. Connally after the *third shot* was fired. The third shot, according to our tentative deductions to this point, caused a massive exit wound in the top of the President's head which, as substantiated by other eyewitness testimony, accounts for the source of the "brain matter" which appeared in Mrs. Kennedy's hands.

This sequence of actions and utterances tends to indicate that Mrs. Kennedy's first utterance (a part of the *res gestae* of the *first shot*) resulted from something other than "her having his brains in her hands." The cause of the first utterance will come to light when we hear Mrs. Kennedy's testimony.

Mr. Specter. From that point forward you say you had your eyes to the front so you did not have a chance —

A — Yes, because I had him, and I really didn't think about looking back. . . .

. . . . .

Mr. Dulles. I just have one more question. Mrs. Connally, on one point your testimony differs from a good many others as to the timing of the shots. I think you said that there seemed to be more time between the second and third than between the first and the second; is that your recollection?

A — Yes.

(The time lapse from Z-206 to Z-236 measures 1.6 seconds; from Z-236 to Z-313 measures 4.2 seconds.)

End of Mrs. Connally's testimony.

Mrs. Connally's testimony parallels our investigative control schedule as follows:

Control point	Elapsed time	Mrs. Connally's key testimony.
Station "C"		Said, "Mr. President, you can't say Dallas doesn't love you."
CPZ-206	Zero	Heard "frightening noise" from her right. Looked over right shoulder. Heard Governor Connally start to cry, "Oh! no, no." Heard Mrs. Kennedy start to cry, "Jack! they've killed my husband."

148

CPZ-225 1.0 sec. While looking back over right shoulder saw President with hands at throat level and "sort of nothing" expression on his face. Watched him "just sort of slump down."

CPZ-236 1.6 sec. Heard second shot and saw Governor Connally "crumple like a wounded animal to the right."
Heard Governor Connally exclaim, "My God, they're going to kill us all."
Pulled Governor Connally over into her arms.

CPZ-313 5.8 sec. Heard and felt third shot.
Saw human matter splatter all over them.
Felt sensation of spent buckshot falling about.
Heard Mrs. Kennedy utter (and repeat several times), "They have killed my husband. I have his brains in my hands."
Recognized that Governor Connally was still alive.
Started talking to him quietly.

Investigative analysis and check of Mrs. Connally's testimony.

We find Mrs. Connally to be an excellent witness. Her account of what took place within two yards of her position in the presidential limousine is plausible and well within the realm of technical possibility. We find Mrs. Connally to be an alert and perceptive person who exhibited unusual self-control and presence of mind throughout the entire shocking

149

circumstance of the assassination. She appears to have been the one person who was listening rather than talking during the shooting episode. Her testimony is positive, straightforward, and has unbroken continuity throughout the circumstance under investigation.

Her eyewitness account checks closely with all of our control points both as to apparent happenings and their sequential order of occurrence. Although poorly questioned on the item, her estimate that the time interval between the second and third shots was longer than the time interval between the first and second shots is in accord with our calculated time intervals.

Her testimony that she heard Governor Connally start to utter, "Oh, no, no, no," immediately following the "frightening noise," as she qualifies the initial rifle report, is to be given greater weight (for reasons previously discussed) than Governor Connally's own recollection that he uttered it after he had been struck by the second shot.

Her testimony that Mrs. Kennedy started to utter, "Jack, they have killed my husband," immediately after the initial rifle report but before the second shot, is strong evidence by virtue of its being a part of the *res gestae* of the initial rifle report and Mrs. Kennedy's observations of her husband instantly thereafter. It is critical evidence that will be used later.

Where it applies, Mrs. Connally's testimony fully corroborates our tentative deductions to this point.

Taking into account all evidence and testimony that we have checked through our investigative control system to this point, we conclude that:

1. An initial rifle shot occurred when the presidential

150

limousine was at the road position designated as our CPZ-206. President Kennedy was struck by this bullet and reacted to its effect.

2. A second rifle shot occurred when the presidential limousine had moved to the road position designated as our CPZ-236. This rifle bullet passed clean through President Kennedy's neck and continued on to strike Governor Connally in the back, right wrist, and left thigh, in that order, ending up spent as a whole bullet in Governor Connally's clothing. This bullet was fired from the Mannlicher-Carcano rifle found on the sixth floor of the Texas School Book Depository. It was fired from an elevated position rearward of the presidential limousine.

3. A third rifle shot occurred when the presidential limousine was at the road position designated as our CPZ-313. This rifle bullet struck the President in the back of the head and, after transiting the interior of his brain cavity, generated a massive "blowout" type exit wound in the top of his head. The bullet, whole or fragmented, passed out of the President's skull case through the massive exit wound. This bullet was fired from a position rearward of the presidential limousine.

Author's Comment: The foregoing deductions might seem to parallel those causing the Commission's dilemma as explained in Chapter V. We have three shots, the second causing the President's neck wound and Governor Connally's multiple wounds, and the third causing the President's massive head wound.

It would appear that we are at that critical crossroads from which the Commission's investigators set out in search of "a bullet that missed." However, our employment of controlled procedures has brought us to this critical point with the investigative knowledge

151

that President Kennedy was struck by, and reacted to, the bullet from the initial rifle shot — and that the wound received *was not a neck wound.*

Circumstantially, and in very broad outline, we have solved the mystery of the bullets.

Three bullets were fired at the President; he was struck by all three. The first struck him and caused him to react physically as we have described. The second passed clean through his neck and continued on to strike Governor Connally. The third penetrated his skull from the rear and generated a massive head wound as it exited.

The second bullet was fired from an elevated position rearward of the presidential limousine, namely from the sixth-floor window of the Depository, and it was fired out of a Mannlicher-Carcano rifle found on the sixth floor of the Depository. The third bullet was fired from a position directly rearward of the presidential limousine, which would localize the position to a south window of the Depository that looks directly down the Elm Street straightaway.

Investigatively speaking, we have arrived at the point where we must shift the emphasis from what we have already determined to those things which, as yet, are not fully explained and fitted into the solution.

There is to be no change in our control procedure but, as evidence and testimony become less direct and specific, we will have to draw on our technical knowledge and experience to fit these unexplained items of material evidence and testimony into the broad outline of the solution that we have determined to this point.

Obviously, our most critical unexplained circumstance is the path and effect of the first bullet fired at the President at our CPZ-206. Our most pressing investigative ques-

152

tion becomes, "What was the nature of the wound inflicted on the President by this first bullet that struck him?"

Lacking the answer to this question, we are unable to determine whether the first or third bullet killed the President. We do know that the neck wound inflicted by the second bullet was not a mortal wound and that the wound inflicted by the third bullet would have been a mortal wound — provided the President had not already been mortally wounded by the first bullet.

We note that we have no investigative accounting for two large bullet fragments found in the driver's compartment of the presidential limousine, although it has been determined ballistically that both fragments were fired from the Mannlicher-Carcano rifle found on the sixth floor of the Depository, and both are similar in type to the blunt-nosed full metal-jacketed bullet recovered from Governor Connally's clothing and the unfired bullet found in the chamber of the Mannlicher-Carcano rifle. We are aware that it cannot be determined ballistically whether these two large fargments, a nose section and a base section, represent one bullet or two bullets.

We have no investigative accounting for a small star crack on the interior of the windshield and a dent in the interior chrome border of the windshield, both located immediately above and slightly to the right of the driver's position in the front compartment of the presidential limousine.

Using evidence and determinations at hand, we can make several logical straight-line deductions. Autopsy disclosed that there were only two points at which bullets entered the President's body — the back of his neck and the back of his head. The neck bullet exited through a small hole in the front of his throat; the bullet entering his head exited through a massive hole in the top of his skull.

We have established that the second bullet struck the President in the back of the neck, and the third bullet struck him in the back of the head, which accounts for the order in which he received these wounds. We have also established that the President was struck and wounded by the first shot.

It follows, logically and conclusively, that the only place that the first bullet could have struck the President was on the top of his head somewhere within the surface area obliterated by the massive head wound.

This deduction also gives us an affirmative answer to our question regarding the possibility of the massive head wound being a multiple wound, i.e., caused by two bullets.

Even with these somewhat startling deductions at hand, our investigation is by no means complete.

We call our next witness.

———————

Testimony of Secret Service Agent Roy H. Kellerman, who was seated in the front compartment of the presidential limousine on the right side, directly ahead of Governor Connally.

Author's Comment: It is to be noted that Agent Kellerman's position in the presidential limousine was somewhat closed off from the rear section of the vehicle. He sat low between a high windshield to his front and the equally high limousine compartment panel window directly behind him. Also, there was a right sidepanel glass extending forward about eight inches from the compartment panel. Sitting as he was down between these two high panels with his right shoulder in a glass corner, he was blanked off

154

somewhat from sounds coming directly from the front or directly from the rear. He would hear Governor Connally least of all, due to the compartment panel intervening immediately between them.

. . . . .   (Wit-pp. 51-54)

Mr. Specter. Describe the occupants of that car (the presidential limousine), indicating their positions, if you can, please.

A — Yes. The President — President Kennedy sat on the right rear seat. Next to him on the left seat was Mrs. Kennedy. On the right jump seat in front of President Kennedy was Governor Connally. On the left jump seat in front of Mrs. Kennedy was Mrs. Connally. I sat on the right passenger seat of the driver's seat, and Special Agent William Greer drove the vehicle.

Mr. Specter. How far were you behind the lead car?

A — As we turned off Houston onto Elm (station "C") and made the short little dip to the left going down grade, as I said, we were away from buildings, and were — there was a sign on the side of the road which I don't recall what it was or what it said, but we no more than passed that and you are out in the open, and there is a report like a firecracker, pop. (CPZ-206) And I turned my head to the right because whatever this noise was I was sure that it came from the right and perhaps into the rear, and as I turned my head to the right to view whatever it was or see whatever it was, I heard a voice from the back seat and I firmly believe it was the President's, "My God, I am hit," and I turned around and he has got his hands up here like this (about CPZ-225).

Mr. Specter. Indicating right hand up toward his neck?

155

A — That is right, sir. In fact, both hands were up in that direction (after CPZ-225).

Senator Cooper. Which side of his neck?

A — Beg pardon?

Senator Cooper. Which side of his neck?

A — Both hands were up, sir; this one is like this here and here we are with the hands —

Mr. Specter. Indicating the left hand is up above the head.

A — In the collar section.

Mr. Specter. As you are positioning yourself in the witness chair, your right hand is up with the finger at the ear level as if clutching from the right of the head; would that be an accurate description of the position you pictured there? NOTE: Again we see Mr. Specter leading the witness to describe clutching at the preconceived throat wound.

A — Yes. Good. There was enough for me to verify that the man was hit. So, in the same motion I came right back and grabbed the speaker and said to the driver, "Let's get out of here; we are hit," and grabbed the mike and I said, "Lawson, this is Kellerman," — this is Lawson, who is in the front car. "We are hit; get us to the hospital immediately." Now, in the seconds that I talked just now, a flurry of shells come into the car (CPZ-313). I then looked back and this time Mr. Hill, who was riding on the left front bumper of our followup car, was on the back trunk of our car; the President was sideways down in the back seat. (after CPZ-313)

Mr. Specter. Indicating on his left side?

A — Right; just like I am here.

Mr. Specter. You mean, correct, left side?

A — Correct; yes, sir. Governor Connally by that time is lying flat backwards into her lap — Mrs. Connally —and she was lying flat over him.

156

Mr. Specter. Who was lying flat over him?

A — Mrs. Connally was lying flat over the Governor.

Mr. Specter. You say that you turned to your right immediately after you heard a shot?

A — Yes, sir.

Mr. Specter. What was the reason for your reacting to your right?

A — That was the direction that I heard this noise, pop.

Mr. Specter. Do you have a reaction as to the height from which the noise came?

A — No; honestly, I do not.

Representative Ford. (member of the Commission) Was there any reaction that you noticed on the part of Greer when the noise was noticed by you?

A — You are referring, Mr. Congressman, to the reaction to get this car out of there?

Representative Ford. Yes.

A — Mr. Congressman, I have driven that car many times and I never cease to be amazed even to this day with the weight of the automobile plus the power that is under the hood; we just literally jumped out of the God-damn road.

Representative Ford. As soon as this noise was heard, or as soon as you transmitted this message to Lawson?

A — As soon as I transmitted to the driver first as I went to Lawson. I just leaned sideways to him and said, "Let's get out of here. We are hit."

Representative Ford. That comment was made to Greer; not to Lawson?

A — Yes, sir; that is right.

Representative Ford. And the subsequent message was to Lawson?

A — Correct. That is right.

Mr. Specter. With relationship to that first noise that you have described, when did you hear the voice?

A — His voice?

Mr. Specter. We will start with his voice.

A — OK. From the noise of which I was in the process of turning to determine where it was or what it was, it carried on right then (after firecracker, pop, at CPZ-206). Why I am so positive, gentlemen, that it was his voice — there is only one man in that back seat that was from Boston, and the accents carried very clearly.

Mr. Specter. Well, had you become familiar with the President's voice prior to that day?

A — Yes; very much so.

Mr. Specter. And what was the basis for your becoming familiar with his voice prior to that day?

A — I had been with him for 3 years.

Mr. Specter. And had you talked with him on a very frequent basis during the course of that association?

A — He was a very free man to talk to; yes. He knew most all of the men, most everybody who worked in the White House as well as everywhere, and he would call you.

Mr. Specter. And from your experience would you say that you could recognize the voice?

A — Very much, sir; I would.

Mr. Specter. Now, I think you may have answered this, but I want to pinpoint just when you heard that statement which you have attributed to President Kennedy in relationship to the sound which you described as a firecracker.

A — This noise which I attribute as a firecracker, when this occurred (CPZ-206) and I am in the process of determining where it comes because I am sure it came off my right rear somewhere; the voice broke in right then.

Author's Comment: The reader's attention is directed

158

to the unusual acoustical circumstances that existed for Agent Kellerman at this moment. As has been noted, he was sitting down between the windshield to his front and the high compartment panel window immediately behind him. Also, it is to be remembered that the limousine was moving at 10 to 12 mph and there were many other motorcade sounds attending.

The "firecracker, pop" caused Agent Kellerman to turn to the right in search of the source of the sound. At this same instant, Governor Connally, according to Mrs. Connally's testimony, was loudly voicing the ejaculation, "Oh, no, no, no," and was, as indicated in Z-222, turned to the right also searching for the source of a rifle report.

Assuming, for test purposes, that President Kennedy did utter, "God! I'm hit" the instant after he was hit at CPZ-206, he would have been facing about half right and his voice would have had its main projection in a direction forward and slightly to the right of the limousine.

Governor Connally would not have heard the President because he, himself, was voicing, "Oh, no, no, no," and it is not likely that either Mrs. Kennedy or Mrs. Connally would have heard the President because they were facing forward or to the left and they both testify to having heard Governor Connally's ejaculation clearly.

Agent Kellerman would not have heard Governor Connally's ejaculation clearly because of the high intervening compartment window panel and because Governor Connally was voicing outward to the right — from a moving vehicle.

Considering the acoustical arrangement and Agent Kellerman's personal responsibilities towards the President, it is not surprising that he would hear clearly the President's voice, which was being projected forward past the one opening through which sound could come to him from his right or from overhead, and not Governor Connally's voice which was directly blocked off by the intervening panel.

Actually, Agent Kellerman may have heard Gover-

159

nor Connally's ejaculation but, as discussed earlier, the human ear hears all attendant sounds simultaneously, but the audio center in the brain tunes up the sound it senses that its owner wants to hear — and, certainly, Agent Kellerman desperately wanted to both see and hear President Kennedy to see how he was faring.

Mr. Specter. At about the same time?

A — That is correct, sir. That is right.

Mr. Specter. Now, did President Kennedy say anything beside, "My God, I am hit."

A — That is the last words he said, sir.

Mr. Specter. Did Mrs. Kennedy say anything at that specific time?

A — Mr. Specter, there was an awful lot of confusion in that back seat. She did a lot of talking which I can't recall all the phrases.

Mr. Specter. Well, pinpoint —

A — But after the flurry of shots (after CPZ-313), I recall her saying, "What are they doing to you?" Now again, of course, my comparison of the voice of her speech — certainly, I have heard it many times, and in the car there was conversation she was carrying on through shock, I am sure.

Mr. Specter. Well, going back to the precise time that you heard the President say, "My God, I am hit," do you recollect whether she said anything at that time?

A — No.

Mr. Specter. Whether or not you can recreate what she said?

A — Not that I can recall right then, sir. This statement, or whatever she said, happened after all the shooting was over.

Mr. Specter. All right. Now, you have described hearing a noise which sounded like a firecracker and you have

160

described turning to your right and described hearing the President's voice and, again, what was your next motion, if any, or movement, if any?

A — After I was sure that his statement was right that he was hit, turned from the back . . .

(testimony continues covering trip to hospital)

Secret Service Agent Roy Kellerman's testimony parallels our investigative control schedule as follows:

Control point	Elapsed time	Agent Kellerman's key testimony.
CPZ-206	Zero	Heard "firecracker, pop." Turned to right to see into back through compartment panel window. Heard President utter, "God, I'm hit!" or sounds to that effect.
CPZ-225	1.0 sec.	Recognized by sight that President was hit and had raised hands to collar level. Turned front and grabbed microphone. Leaned toward Greer and said, "Let's get out of here. We're hit!" Transmitted to Lawson (microphone), "We're hit, get us to the hospital immediately."
CPZ-313	5.8 sec.	". . . a flurry of *shells* come into the car." Turned and saw Mr. Hill on back trunk of presidential limousine. Heard Mrs. Kennedy say, "What are they doing to you."

Investigative analysis and check of Agent Kellerman's testimony.

161

We have noted that Agent Kellerman's hearing was blocked off somewhat from the rear compartment.

We find his testimony plausible and within the realm of technical possibility. We note that he was a professionally trained Secret Service Agent with many years of experience and that he had spent three years in assignment as agent in charge of the President's personal safety. As the President's safety was his assigned responsibility, he can be considered to have been unusually alert and perceptive during the early moments of the assassination. However, during the middle moments of the assassination, the continuity of his attention towards the President was broken, necessarily, by the official orders and instructions that he had to give in an effort to get the President out of danger and to a hospital.

> Author's Comment: The Warren Commission investigators had what they thought was a logical reason for disbelieving Agent Kellerman's statement that he had heard the President utter, "My God, I am hit," immediately after the first shot was fired. The reason, in itself, was logical enough. According to the autopsy, the bullet that had passed through the President's neck had also ripped through his windpipe (trachea) just below the voice box thus making it highly improbable that the President had uttered any intelligible sounds after he was struck in the neck. Here again, their preconception that the President's first wound was the neck wound, led the Commission's investigators to discount, if not ignore, this extremely vital testimony.

Agent Kellerman's *eyewitness* testimony fully corroborates other evidence and testimony which has already indicated that President Kennedy was struck by and physically reacted to the bullet fired at him as he came to CPZ-206.

His *earwitness* testimony, however, furnishes far more vital and constructive evidence at this late point in our investigation.

By deductive association, the President's ejaculation, "God! I'm hit," substantiates and corroborates many other circumstances as yet not fully explained.

> Author's Comment: The President's utterance is a part of the *res gestae* of the initial rifle shot and, as circumstances developed, it also became a *dying declaration*. In either definition, it is extremely strong evidence. Fortunately, we have no "preconceptions" that would cause us to discount or ignore Agent Kellerman's testimony. In fact, our controlled procedures have put us in position to make maximum use of this vital piece of evidence.

First, the President tells us in his own words that he was struck by the first bullet. We had previously deduced that the only place this first bullet could have struck the President was on the top of his head somewhere within the surface area obliterated by the massive head wound.

We can now further deduce that this first head wound was not so severe as to have knocked the President senseless and beyond speech, but that the impact effect of the bullet was severe enough to have knocked him forward and to the left and, as we have previously deduced, to have caused him to react reflexively to an unexpected blow on the top of the head and then to further react, by semi-voluntary reflex, in anticipation of a second blow following on the first.

The foregoing automatically limits the wounding effect of this first bullet to something between a crease wound and a shallow lace wound of the scalp. Our previous deductions locate this wound somewhere within the periphery of the scalp area obliterated by the final massive head

163

wound. Autopsy had disclosed that the final bullet caused an exit wound which blew out the upper right section of the President' skull, leaving an oblong hole in the skull and scalp of at least 5 inches on the long fore-and-aft axis.

Typical ballistic reaction tells us that a bullet inflicting a crease or shallow lace wound of the scalp would have to glance or ricochet off the top of the President's head and, though deflected slightly, would maintain its pristine spin characteristic and continue on its high-velocity course as a whole bullet.

We have determined from previous testimony that the rifle report emanated from an elevated position somewhere rearward of the presidential limousine when it was at CPZ-206. It is a logical assumption, considering the short gun range of 58 yards, that the bullet came from the same direction as the rifle report.

We have determined that at CPZ-206, the President was looking toward and waving to the people on his right. We note that this exposes the upper right side of his head to a bullet fired from the sixth-floor window of the Depository.

> Author's Comment: All material evidence, testimony, and data that has come within the reach and purview of our rigid investigative control system, including engineering alignments, ballistic considerations, visual and aural testimony, and material evidence found either at the point from which the bullets were fired or the locations where bullets or bullet fragments were found or persons or things were determined to have been struck, all point or lead, unerringly, to one, and only one, elevated position in rear of the presidential limousine — *the easternmost window of the sixth floor of the Texas School Book Depository.*

A bullet fired from the elevated sixth-floor window that ricochetted off the top of the President's head would have had to deflect upward or to the right, or both, to miss the high compartment panel or windshield of the presidential limousine in order to continue, uninterrupted, on its high-velocity course which would have been in the general direction of the Triple Underpass. Also, it would have had to pass just over the heads of Governor Connally and Agent Kellerman.

Investigative analysis tells us that Governor Connally, sitting in the open as he was, would have heard the initial rifle report, the thump of the bullet as it ricochetted off the President's head, and the snap of the bullet passing overhead, as a single accentuated rifle report. Mrs. Connally testifies that she heard it as "a frightening noise."

Agent Kellerman, sitting as he was down between the windshield and the high compartment panel, would have been blocked off somewhat from hearing the rifle report and the wounding thump and, unquestionably, would have heard the snap ("firecracker, pop") of the bullet passing overhead as the primary sound.

Agent Kellerman's description of the sound of the initial rifle report as a "firecracker, pop" not only corroborates the timing of the initial rifle report but it further substantiates the ballistic certainty that the ricochetting bullet passed close over his head as it continued on its course towards the Triple Underpass.

The very fact of the President's utterance substantiates our previous determination that the President was not struck in the neck (throat) by the first bullet, and thus rendered incapable of intelligible speech. This, by correlation, more firmly establishes our deductive conclusion that the President's neck wound was his second wound which occurred at CPZ-236.

The President's utterance also gives us a deductive lead on the two large bullet fragments.

We have determined that there were three rifle reports and we have, as material evidence, three expended cartridge cases found on the floor at the sixth-floor window of the Depository. We have ballistic proof that these cartridges were expended (fired) by the Mannlicher-Carcano rifle found on the sixth floor of the Depository. We have just determined that the first bullet ricochetted, as a whole bullet, in the general direction of the Triple Underpass. The second bullet, the famous "single bullet" that hit both the President and Governor Connally, was recovered from the floor of a corridor of Parkland Memorial Hospital in Dallas by a hospital attendant immediately after he had heard it fall to the floor from the hospital stretcher that had been used to convey Governor Connally to the emergency treatment room. This bullet was ballistically proven to have been fired from the Mannlicher-Carcano rifle. The foregoing accounts for the bullets out of two of the three expended cartridge cases found on the floor near the sixth-floor window.

We have, as material evidence, two large bullet fragments found in the front compartment of the presidential limousine. It has been technically determined that they represent a nose section and a base section of a blunt-nosed, full metal-jacketed rifle bullet identical in type to the bullet recovered from the Governor's hospital stretcher and to the bullet cased in the unexpended cartridge found in the chamber of the Mannlicher-Carcano rifle. We have ballistic proof that both of these large fragments were fired from the Mannlicher-Carcano rifle.

All of the foregoing gives us more than adequate investigative grounds upon which to base a conclusion that the two large bullet fragments represent *only one bullet,*

166

and that it was the bullet that struck the President in the back of the head at CPZ-313 and penetrated his brain.

We can further deduce that this third bullet fragmented (sectionalized) on passing through the President's skull and then vented out of the brain case in fragments as the result (or possibly the cause) of the blowout effect through the top of the President's head. Inherent in the foregoing deduction is the ballistic certainty that this "penetrating bullet" caused an increase in pressure in the President's brain case.

Due either to residual ballistic velocity or the "blowout effect" causing the massive exit wound, or both, the two large sections and all other fragments of the bullet continued forward toward the front of the presidential limousine at various velocities until the combined effects of relative wind (speed of the limousine) and the force of gravity caused the two large fragments to arc downward and strike the inside of the windshield just to the right of the driver, Special Agent Greer. From here, they were deflected downward into the front compartment where they were found. This accounts for both the damage done to the interior surface of the windshield and to its upper chrome border, and for the locations of these impact points on the inner surface of the windshield. Engineering-wise, a nearly straight line can be drawn from the sixth-floor window through the President's head to the impact points on the interior of the windshield.

It is a ballistic certainty that the other smaller fragments of this bullet, depending on their ballistic mass, configuration, and velocity, either fell immediately into the rear section of the limousine or continued on forward over the windshield to arc downward and strike the ground or pavement at random points ahead of the presidential limousine in the general direction of the center of the Triple Underpass.

Agent Kellerman's testimony that a "flurry of *shells* came into the car" at CPZ-313, tends to substantiate our deductions regarding the path and final position of the two major fragments of the third bullet.

Referring back to previous testimony, we quote Mrs. Connally's statement regarding the effects of the third bullet. Quote: "The third shot that I heard I felt, it felt like *spent buckshot* falling all over us, and then, of course, I too could see that it was matter, brain tissue, or whatever, just human matter, all over the car and both of us."

> Author's Comment: Agents of the FBI found three small lead particles, weighing between seven-tenths and nine-tenths of a grain each, on the rug underneath the left jump seat which had been occupied by Mrs. Connally. As investigators, we marvel at the accuracy with which Mrs. Connally described the ballistic phenomenon that actually occurred.
>
> A trained investigator would note further that the combined weight of the two large fragments found in the front compartment and those found under Mrs. Connally's seat was only 65 grains. The whole bullet before it disintegrated weighed 160 grains. It becomes a ballistic certainty that some 95 grains of various sized fragments with various velocities flew out over the windshield and hit the ground or pavement at varying distances in a fan out in front of the presidential limousine in the general direction of the center of the Triple Underpass.
>
> As experienced investigators, we would *anticipate* that some of their impact effects would be reported by any eyewitnesses who might be located in that general area.

168

Taking into account the results of all controlled investigative actions to this point, we conclude that:

1. The Mannlicher-Carcano rifle was fired from the sixth-floor window of the Depository when the presidential limousine was moving over the Elm Street road position designated as CPZ-206. This bullet struck and ricochetted off the top of President Kennedy's head. It was deflected upward and slightly to the right. It maintained its pristine characteristic and continued on its high-velocity course in the general direction of the Triple Underpass.

2. A second bullet was fired from the Mannlicher-Carcano rifle approximately 1.6 seconds after the preceding shot when the presidential limousine was moving over the road position designated as CPZ-236. This bullet passed clean through President Kennedy's neck and continued on its downward course to strike Governor Connally in the back, right wrist and left thigh, in that order, and ended up spent as a whole bullet in Governor's Connally's clothing.

3. A third bullet was fired from the Mannlicher-Carcano rifle approximately 4.2 seconds after the preceding (second) shot, when the presidential limousine was moving over the road position designated as CPZ-313. This bullet struck the President in the back of the head, entered his brain cavity and, by either interior impact effect or "confined liquid" overpressure effect, or both, generated a massive "blowout" type exit wound in the top of his head. The bullet fragmented (sectionalized) on entering and the resulting fragments passed out of the President's skull case through the massive exit wound. Two major fragments of this third bullet were cast into the forward compartment of the presidential limousine, three nominal sized

169

fragments fell into the rear compartment, and other fragments of unknown size flew forward over the limousine in the general direction of the Triple Underpass.

At this point, it can be seen that only two items remain which require further detailed investigation.

1. The physical wounding (bone and tissue damaging) effect of the first bullet to strike the President.

2. The resultant weakening of the President's brain encasement (skull and scalp) and the degree to which this weakening would induce "confined liquid" explosive effect and cause a "blowout" type exit wound at the "weak spot."

We are unable, for lack of direct evidence, to determine the amount of damage done to the President's skull and its encasing scalp by the first bullet to strike the President. As a result, we lack the evidence necessary to demonstrate any weakening effect on the President's brain encasement from the first wound, even though we have deduced that the first bullet struck somewhere on the surface area obliterated by the massive wound and that the severity of the wound lies somewhere between a crease wound and a shallow lace wound of the scalp.

All of the foregoing results from the investigative fact that up to now we lack *prima facie* evidence of the first wound itself!

In plain and simple terms, no one has yet testified to actually having seen the wound.

We call our final witness.

———————————

Testimony of Mrs. John F. Kennedy, wife of the President of the United States of America, who was seated on

170

the left side of the rear seat of the presidential limousine.

Mrs. Kennedy was questioned on June 5, 1964 at her residence at 3017 N Street N.W., Washington, D.C., by J. Lee Rankin, General Counsel of the President's Commission. Present were Chief Justice Earl Warren, Chairman of the Commission; and Robert F. Kennedy, Attorney General of the United States of America.

(Wit-pp. 1-4)

The Chairman. The Commission will be in order.

Mrs. Kennedy, the Commission would just like to have you say in your own words, in your own way, what happened at the time of the assassination of the President. Mr. Rankin will ask you a few questions, just from the time you left the airport until the time you started for the hospital. And we want it to be brief. We want it to be in your own words and want you to say anything that you feel is appropriate to that occasion.

Would you be sworn, please, Mrs. Kennedy? . . .

A — I do.

The Chairman. Would you be seated.

Mr. Rankin. State your name for the record.

A — Jacqueline Kennedy.

Mr. Rankin. And you are the widow of the former President Kennedy?

A — That is right.

(intervening questions and answers beginning with arrival at Love Field, Dallas, on 22 November 1963)

. . . . . .

Mr. Rankin. As you got into the main street of Dallas were there very large crowds on all the streets?

A — Yes.

Mr. Rankin. And you waved to them and proceeded down the street in the motorcade?

A — Yes. And with the motorcade, you know, I usually would be waving mostly to the left side and he was waving mostly to the right, which is one reason you are not looking at each other very much. And it was terribly hot. Just blinding all of us.

Mr. Rankin. Now, do you remember as you turned off of the main street onto Houston Street?

A — I don't know the name of the street.

Mr. Rankin. That is that one block before you get to the Depository building.

A — Well, I remember whenever it was, Mrs. Connally said, "We will soon be there." We could see a tunnel (the Triple Underpass) in front of us. Everything was really slow then. And I remember thinking it would be so cool under that tunnel.

Mr. Rankin. And then you do remember as you turned off of Houston onto Elm right by the Depository Building (Station "C")?

A — Well, I don't know the names of the streets, but I suppose right by the Depository is what you are talking about?

Mr. Rankin. Yes; that is the street that sort of curves as you go down under the underpass.

A — Yes; well, that is when she (Mrs. Connally) said to President Kennedy, "You certainly can't say that the people of Dallas haven't given you a nice welcome."

Mr. Rankin. What did he say?

A — I think he said — I don't know if I remember it or I have read it, "No, you certainly can't," or something. And you know then the car was very slow and there weren't very many people around.

172

And then — do you want me to tell you what happened?

Mr. Rankin. Yes; if you would, please.

A — You know, there is always noise in a motorcade and there are always motorcycles besides us, a lot of them backfiring. So I was looking to the left. I guess there was a noise, but it didn't seem like any different noise really because there is so much noise, motorcycles and things. But then suddenly Governor Connally was yelling, "Oh, no, no, no." (between CPZ-206 and about Z-220)

Mr. Rankin. Did he turn toward you?

A — No; I was looking this way, to the left, and I heard these terrible noises. You know. And my husband never made any sound. So I turned to the right. (Z-222 shows Mrs. Kennedy already looking toward the President.) And all I remember is seeing my husband. he had this sort of quizzical look on his face, and his hand was up, it must have been his left hand. And just as I turned and looked at him (well before our CPZ-225) *I could see a piece of his skull and I remember it was flesh colored.* I remember thinking he just looked as if he had a slight headache. And I just remember seeing that. No blood or anything.

And then he sort of did this (indicating), put his hand to his forehead and fell in my lap.

And then I just remember falling on him and saying, "Oh, no, no, no," I mean, "Oh, my God, they have shot my husband." And "I love you, Jack," I remember I was shouting. And it just seemed an eternity.

You know, then, there were pictures later on of me climbing out the back, but I don't remember that at all.

Mr. Rankin. Do you remember Mr. Hill coming to try to help on the car?

A — I don't remember anything. I was just down like that.

And finally I remember a voice behind me, or some-

173

thing, and then I remember the people in the front seat, or somebody, finally knew something was wrong, and a voice yelling, which must have been Mr. Hill, "Get to the hospital," or maybe it was Mr. Kellerman, in the front seat. But someone yelling. I was just down and holding him. . . . (reference to massive head wound deleted)

Mr. Rankin. Do you have any recollection of whether there were one or more shots?

> Author's Comment: Mrs. Kennedy's answer to this question is a good example of how unqualified (prior) information can influence and confuse about everybody who hears it — more especially, witnesses. Mrs. Kennedy's recollections of the assassination are seen to be what she actually remembers (which is essentially correct) with an admixture of what she had been led to believe by the Single Bullet Theory, the Commission's erroneous preconception that the neck wound was the first wound, and, possibly, Agent Kellerman's having told her that he had heard the President utter, "My God, I am hit," after the initial rifle report.
>
> It will be to her lasting credit that the First Lady did as well as she did in trying to tell the straight story — as she remembered it. She gave them the all important clue in as clear terms as it can be spoken. Being blinded to it by a preconception, they passed it by, unnoticed!

A — Well, there must have been two because the one that made me turn around was Governor Connally yelling. And it used to confuse me because first I remembered there were three and I used to think my husband didn't make any sound when he was shot. And Governor Connally screamed. And then I read the other day that it was the same shot that hit them both. But I used to think if I only had been looking to the right, I would have seen the first

174

shot hit him, then I could have pulled him down, and then the second shot would not have hit him. But I heard Governor Connally yelling and that made me turn around, and as I turned to the right my husband was doing this (indicating with hand at neck). He was receiving a bullet. And those are the only two I remember.

And I just read there was a third shot. But I don't know.

Just those two.

Mr. Rankin. Do you have any recollection generally of the speed that you were going, not any precise amount.

A — We were really slowing turning the corner. And there were very few people.

Mr. Rankin. And did you stop at any time after the shots, or proceed about the same way?

A — I don't know, because — I don't think we stopped. But there was such confusion. And I was down in the car and everyone was yelling to get to the hospital and you could hear them on the radio, and then suddenly I remember a sensation of enormous speed, which must have been when we took off.

Mr. Rankin. And then from there you proceeded as rapidly as possible to the hospital, is that right?

A — Yes.

Mr. Rankin. Do you recall anyone saying anything else during the time of the shooting?

A — No; there weren't any words. There was just Governor Connally's. And I suppose Mrs. Connally was sort of crying and covering her husband. But I don't remember any words.

And there was a big windshield between — you know — I think. Isn't there? (compartment panel window)

Mr. Rankin. Between the seats.

A — So you know, those poor men in the front, you couldn't hear them.

Mr. Rankin. Can you think of anything more?

The Chairman. No; I think not. I think that is the story and that is what we came for.

We thank you very much, Mrs. Kennedy.

Mr. Rankin. I would just like to ask if you recall Special Agent Kellerman saying anything to you as you came down the street after you turned that corner that you referred to?

A — You mean before the shots?

Mr. Rankin. Yes.

A — Well, I don't, because — you know, it is very hard for them to talk. But I do not remember, just as I don't recall climbing out on the back of the car.

Mr. Rankin. Yes. You have told us what you remember about the entire period as far as you can recall, have you?

A — Yes.

The Chairman. Thank you very much, Mrs. Kennedy.

Mrs. Kennedy's testimony parallels our investigative control schedule as follows:

Control point	Elapsed time	Mrs. Kennedy's key testimony.
Station "C"	. . . .	Heard Mrs. Connally say, "You certainly can't say that the people of Dallas haven't given you a nice welcome." Heard President answer, "No, you certainly can't."

176

CPZ-206	Zero	Heard "these terrible noises." Heard Governor Connally start yelling, "Oh! no, no," while looking left. Reflexively turned right to look at her husband. *"Saw a piece of his skull and it was flesh colored."* Saw a quizzical look on the President's face.
Z-222	0.9 sec.	This Zapruder film frame clearly shows that Mrs. Kennedy has already turned far enough around to be facing the President.
CPZ-225	1.0 sec.	Mrs. Kennedy appears to be looking intently at the President. Saw President put his hand to his fore-
CPZ-236	1.6 sec.	head — "and he fell into my lap."

Author's Comment: We are unable to tie Mrs. Kennedy's testimony into our control schedule after CPZ-236, although the Zapruder film strip shows that she continued to peer at and seemed to be intently scrutinizing the President's face until after he had suffered the massive "blowout" type head wound at CPZ-313. This results, in part, from the "tell it in your own words" type of interrogation given Mrs. Kennedy and the deletion (in our source) of the part of her testimony dealing with her observation of the results of the massive head wound received by the President at CPZ-313.

Investigative analysis and check of Mrs. Kennedy's testimony.

Mrs. Kennedy needs no qualification as a person — her qualities are known throughout the world.

Her testimony, as given to the Commission's interrogators, was best qualified by Mrs. Kennedy herself when she stated, clearly enough, that it had all been a terrible and shocking thing and that what she thought she remembered and what she had been led to believe did not seem to coincide — so, she had become confused. This is not surprising, considering the erroneous schedule of information that had come to her attention after the assassination — but before the interrogation.

Taking the above into full account, we find that her testimony is reasonably clear and in good continuity up to our CPZ-225, which will be sufficient for our purposes here.

Continuing our rigid control of evidence and testimony, it is vital that we determine within very close limits when Mrs. Kennedy turned to the right and looked at the President.

We have several ways by which this can be determined. Mrs. Kennedy testifies that she turned immediately (reflexively) on hearing "these terrible noises" and hearing Governor Connally start to yell, "Oh! no, no." It is to be recalled that our investigative deductions place the start of Governor Connally's ejaculation, "Oh! no, no," well before CPZ-225. This line of deduction puts her turn before CPZ-225.

Our best evidence, however, is Zapruder film frame Z-222 (three frames ahead of our CPZ-225), which is the point at which Mrs. Kennedy comes back into Zapruder camera view, after her having been blocked out by the same intervening road sign that blocked out President Kennedy until CPZ-225.

Z-222 clearly shows Mrs. Kennedy turned toward and apparently looking at the President.

This establishes, beyond any question, that Mrs. Ken-

178

nedy had turned and was looking at the President before Z-222. It follows that she turned and looked at President Kennedy immediately after the first bullet had struck him at CPZ-206. Mrs. Kennedy's own words covering this critical moment are, "And just as I turned and looked at him, *I could see a piece of his skull and it was flesh colored. I remember thinking he just looked as if he had a slight headache. And I remember seeing that. No blood or anything.*"

Correlating with this, we have Mrs. Connally's testimony that she heard Mrs. Kennedy start to utter, "Jack! they've killed my husband," immediately after the first shot — but before the second shot. We have investigatively determined that this utterance by Mrs. Kennedy was a part of the *res gestae* of the first rifle shot and that it must have grown out of the shock encountered by Mrs. Kennedy as she turned and looked at President Kennedy immediately after the first shot. Her utterance, "Jack, they've killed my husband," proves to be entirely compatible with her having turned and received the terrible shock of seeing what she believed to be *a piece of her husband's skull* sticking out of the top of his head! Here, in her utterance, we have not only strong evidence substantiating the fact that the first bullet struck the President, but that it generated a *visible wound* on the top of his head.

Here, in her own testimony, Mrs. Kennedy gives us the vital piece of evidence we have been looking for — *visual evidence of the wounding effect of the first bullet that struck and ricochetted off the top of the President's head.*

What she actually saw, by her description, was a shallow lace wound of the President's scalp. What she identifies as a piece of his skull was a flap of his scalp blown up, or ploughed up, by the bullet as it penetrated to, and then

179

skipped or glanced off, the bony plate of his skull. She did not see a piece of his skull, as the human skull, on momentary exposure, *is pearly white*. The scalp, which is thicker than most people realize, 3/8 of an inch or more, is a flap of skin-covered tissue that appears *flesh colored* when ripped away from the skull and the underside is exposed to view.

It is an investigative certainty, at this point, that a scalp wound was observed by Mrs. Kennedy. The bullet obviously laced through the President's scalp for a distance sufficient to plough up a flap of his scalp, which, due to its direction of exposure, was visible only to Mrs. Kennedy. The President's very thick bushy hair would have momentarily captured any bleeding. No tissue other than filaments of hair would have come out of such a lacing scalp wound.

What does Mrs. Kennedy's testimony tell us? First, it substantiates all of our deductions to this point regarding the first bullet to strike the President. More importantly, it tells us that the first bullet inflicted a lace wound of the President's scalp of sufficient length to have ploughed up and made visible a section of his scalp. This visible scalp flap supports the estimate that the President suffered a degree of concussive effect to both his skull case and to his state of consciousness.

The impact effect of this glancing bullet was sufficient to knock the President forward and to the left and to cause him to reflexively hunch his shoulders, raise his elbows up and forward, and move his hands to a position in front of his face. These reflexive movements indicate that the blow was not of sufficient magnitude to cause instantaneous unconsciousness and total muscular collapse. The fact that he uttered, "God, I'm hit!" after having been struck, further indicates that the momentary concussive effect was intermediate rather than severe.

The degree to which the President was dazed or stunned and the extent of the concussion and skull damage, within the limits expressed above, must remain problematical. However, with the lace wound of the scalp now in evidence, we can conclude that the capacity of the President's brain encasement to absorb or withstand high momentary pressures generated by the penetration of a high-velocity bullet was reduced somewhat at the site of the lace wound on the right side of the top of his head.

The combination of a weakened skull encasement from the lace wound, over-pressure from high-velocity rifle bullet penetration, and interior skull damage from the transiting bullet fragments, makes it a near certainty that a confined liquid "blowout" type wound would occur at the weak spot on the right side of the top of the President's head.

The resulting wound and the attendant "very loud and clear" sound give every evidence of having been generated by explosive forces.

Photographic evidence beginning instantly at CPZ-313 clearly shows (by rate of discharge and volume of visible matter) that the exit wound incurred at this point was explosive in nature.

The testimony of Governor and Mrs. Connally, both as to sounds and effects, points to a "blowout" type wound.

In short, a preponderance of evidence exists to establish that the third bullet penetrated the President's brain case and, by a combination of dynamic, ballistic and physical factors, caused a "blowout" type exit wound of explosive proportions that generated a massive exit wound at the site of the lace wound caused by the first bullet to strike the President.

181

Mrs. Kennedy's testimony has given us the final vital piece of evidence that was required to solve the mystery of the bullets, and, thereby, has made it possible for us to accomplish our objective.

The Solution

We announced at the beginning of our joint investigation that we were going to determine how John Fitzgerald Kennedy, then President of the United States of America, was killed at high noon in Dealey Plaza, Dallas, Texas, on 22 November 1963.

Using sound investigative procedures and rigid control of material evidence and testimony, we have determined, beyond any question of a doubt, that it occurred as follows:

At approximately 12:30 P.M. CST, on 22 November 1963, after the presidential limousine had turned off Houston Street and proceeded approximately 135 feet down Elm Street at approximately 11 miles per hour in the direction of the Triple Underpass, President Kennedy was fired upon from the easternmost sixth-floor window on the south face of the Texas School Book Depository, a gun range of about 58 yards, by a person using a 6.50 m/m Mannlicher-Carcano military rifle mounted with a telescopic sight. This first bullet struck the President a glancing blow on the right side of the top of his head and, with only slightly diminished velocity and nominal deflection, ricochetted off over the heads of Governor Connally and Secret Service Agent Kellerman in the direction of the Triple Underpass.

The impact of this glancing bullet knocked the President forward and slightly to the left and generated a visible lace wound of his scalp on the line of its glancing impact.

182

The President retained consciousness and uttered, "God, I'm hit!" or sounds to that effect.

Approximately 1.6 seconds after the first bullet had struck the President, he was fired upon a second time by the same rifleman at a gun range of about 68 yards. This second bullet passed clean through the President's neck and continued on its downward course to strike Governor Connally in the back, right wrist, and left thigh, in that order. The spent whole bullet remained in Governor Connally's clothing.

The impact of this second bullet as it passed through the President's neck caused only a slight reactionary movement of his head to the left. Its impact on Governor Connally caused him to crumple instantaneously to his right.

Approximately 4.2 seconds after the second shot and at a range of about 90 yards, the President was fired upon a third time by the same rifleman. This third bullet struck the President in the back of his head and, in combination with the wounding effect of the first bullet, generated a "blowout" type exit wound of massive proportions at the site of the first wound, which obliterated all evidence of the first wound.

This third bullet sectionalized as it entered the President's skull and blew out in fragments through the massive exit wound. These fragments shot out in various ballistic patterns in the direction of travel of the presidential limousine.

The impact of the third bullet caused the President's head to move forward. Instantly thereafter, the reactionary propulsive effect of the "blowout" type exit wound caused his head to move backward and to the left.

183

The third bullet was the final bullet fired at the President.

The President was killed at the instant the third bullet struck him!

One assassin — three shots — three hits — and no misses!

It was as uncomplicated as that.

It is to be recalled that the primary objective of this book was to defend, in fact to substantiate, the principal conclusion set forth by the President's Commission that one assassin, acting alone, fired three bullets at the President, thereby killing him. Inherent in the foregoing was support of the contingent conclusion that Governor Connally got caught in the same line of fire.

The foregoing resolution of the mystery of the bullets provides this substantiation — and defense.

The reader is left to judge the sufficiency of the legal premise that it provides to sustain an indictment against the lone rifleman who shot and killed the President.

The following attendant results were predicted:

a. The President's Commission would be vindicated (somewhat).

b. The eyewitness accounts rendered by Governor and Mrs. John B. Connally, Jr., would be shown to have been true and correct in major detail.

c. The eyewitness accounts rendered by Mrs. John F. Kennedy and Secret Service Agent Roy H. Kellerman would be shown to have provided the final vital clues that solved the mystery of the bullets.

184

d. The witch hunt for other assassins would be brought to a halt.

Having joined in the investigaiton, the reader already will have formed judgments regarding the foregoing.

We agree, as associates, that we have accomplished what we set out to do. However, being experienced investigators, we cannot fail to note, in closing this investigation, that there are a number of questions left unanswered.

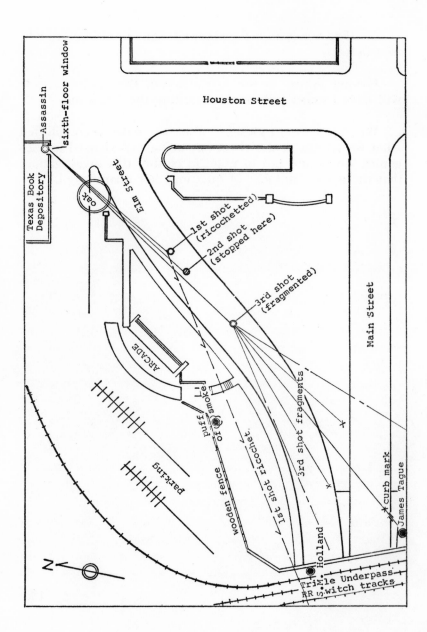

Chapter IX

SOME UNANSWERED QUESTIONS

Sound investigative procedures and the application of rigid control of evidence have solved the mystery of the bullets in routine order.

By now, the reader will have sensed another advantage gained through the use of good investigative control — it screens out irrelevant and erroneous evidence as effectively as it identifies and checks sound evidence. When properly applied, it shields the working investigator from the many unrelated or related but irrelevant incidents and happenings which are bound to be observed by eyewitnesses viewing such a swift and moving scene.

Once the solution is announced, however, the pattern changes and the investigator finds himself immediately called upon, and rightly so, to account for and explain concomitant circumstances and phenomena which, on first view, seem to oppose the solution or remain unexplained in the face of it.

A correct solution welcomes questions, provided they are *bona fide* questions regarding true and related incidents and phenomena, because proper investigation into them can bring forth only additional evidence in support of the solution.

The author, like the President's Commission, will retire into the sanctuary of literary silence on the publication of this document. In view of this, it is both timely and expedient to entertain several unanswered questions before closing this investigation.

It is to be recalled that in solving the mystery, it was not necessary to investigatively trace each bullet beyond a certain point in its flight. To insure against committing a fault assigned the Commission, that of failing to determine the actual path, effect and sequential position of each bullet, we will here consider, as unanswered questions, the continuing paths and effects of the three bullets to their ballistic terminations.

The First Bullet

Where did the bullet go that ricochetted off the top of the President's head and continued, per the solution, in the general direction of the Triple Underpass?

It is to be recalled that it was not necessary to determine the course of this bullet beyond its "firecracker, pop" over Agent Kellerman's head to the right — which established the ballistic fact that it had continued past the President after striking him.

A Mr. S. M. Holland was standing on the railroad

188

overpass (Triple Underpass) above Elm Street during the assassination. The Grassy Knoll and arcade were slightly to his left in the foreground. He was looking back up Elm Street on just about the reverse arc that the assassin was looking down it from the sixth-floor window of the Depository.

Mr. Holland testifies (to the Commission) that, "I heard a noise like a firecracker and I looked toward the arcade and trees and saw a puff of smoke come from the trees — and then I heard three more shots after the first shot (firecracker sound) but that was the only puff of smoke that I saw." All this he saw and heard while the presidential limousine was rolling down Elm Street towards him from the direction of the Depository.

Referring back to our investigative control schedule, the presidential limousine was at CPZ-206 when the first bullet to strike the President ricochetted. Agent Kellerman testifies that the sound of the passing bullet (a "firecracker, pop") was to the right of him and *perhaps* to the rear. Considering the relative positions of Agent Kellerman and the President, this would indicate that the course of the ricochetting bullet was towards the *north end* of the railroad overpass — where Mr. Holland was standing.

Ballistically, a bullet precedes the sound of its rifle report by an increasing interval of time as the distance increases between the listener who hears the bullet "snap" overhead and the point at which the rifle was fired. Mr. Holland, standing over 500 feet from where the Mannlicher-Carcano rifle was fired, would have heard the firecracker-snap of its bullet passing overhead at least 1/3 of a second before he heard the following report of the rifle. (See map plan page 186.)

He testifies that this first "firecracker" sound came from his left, which drew his attention to the arcade and trees in his left foreground — where he then saw a puff of smoke.

Investigative experience and rigid control of evidence would rule out attaching any significance to the puff of smoke. We know that all modern powder is smokeless. More important, however, is the ballistic evidence indicating that Mr. Holland's attention was drawn to the wooden stockade fence (where the puff of smoke was seen) by the *sound of a bullet* passing overhead to his left rather than by the sound of a rifle report. It is investigatively evident why he would sense that the original sound (the passing bullet) came from the direction of the arcade — it did!

After hearing the initial sound to the left and then (by coincidence) seeing a puff of smoke (however generated) in the area from which the sound had come, it is not difficult to understand why Mr. Holland would conclude that something had been fired from that point.

With the solution and the investigative control schedule to guide on, Mr. Holland would experience little difficulty in aligning his observations with the ballistic facts of the case. Also, Mr. Holland will realize something else — how close he came to being hit by this ricochetting bullet!

But where did the bullet ultimately go? With Mr. Holland's testimony, it can be tracked past the north end of the Triple Underpass heading westward. From this point, the Law of Gravity would take over, so — it lies spent somewhere beyond the Triple Underpass to the west. If it is someday found, it can be tested ballistically and will prove to have been fired from the Mannlicher-Carcano rifle that killed the President.

The Second Bullet

What was the ballistic path and wounding effect of the

second bullet after it had passed through President Kennedy's neck and sped on, at diminished velocity and with nominal right deflection, in the direction of Governor Connally's back?

It is to be recalled that our investigation established that this second bullet had passed clean through President Kennedy's neck which established the ballistic certainty that it had continued its forward and slightly downward course in the direction of Governor Connally's back. This, with other strong evidence, permitted the logical (but unspecified) conclusion that the bullet then had struck Governor Connally in the back, right wrist and left thigh, in that order, and had ended up spent in his clothing.

Wound trauma evidence gained during Governor Connally's interrogation, as corroborated and expertized by Doctors Shaw and Gregory (pp. 127-128 this book, and Wit-pp. 21-28), described the wounds as follows: A bullet entered Governor Connally's back at a point on the right shoulder just lateral to the shoulder blade and just above and medial (inward from) the crease formed by the armpit, the arm against the chest wall. It entered through a small neat hole typical of an entrance wound, penetrated to and shattered a rib, and exited through a ragged hole about two inches in diameter in his chest just below the right nipple. His right wrist was pierced by a projectile *which entered from the back of the wrist,* fracturing bones of the wrist.

> NOTE: Shreds of cloth from Governor Connally's coat were found in this wound on the back of the wrist further identifying it as an entrance wound.

The projectile passed through his wrist, exiting through a small wound in the front (palm side) of his wrist.

191

The front of his left thigh, at a point about 5 inches above the knee, received a flesh wound measuring 1½ inches by ½ inch on the skin surface which penetrated tissue to a depth of less than one inch (muscle tissue was not reached).

Referring back to our investigative control schedule, we note that the presidential limousine was very close to CPZ-236 when the second shot (the so-called Single Bullet) was fired. Our formal investigation determined that at this point the President was in the posture necessary to receive the *seemingly rising* neck wound, and Governor Connally, after first having turned to the right, was facing to the front in the process of turning back around to the left, when he felt the bullet strike him in the back.

Zapruder film frames Z-230 on to our CPZ-236 clearly indicate that Governor Connally was grasping the brim of his felt hat with the fingers of his right hand, back of his hand facing his right shoulder and held at about the level of his right arm pit, at the moment he was struck.

With all the foregoing data, evidence, and testimony to go on, the tracing of the path and sequential effects of the bullet as it inflicted Governor Connally's wounds becomes elementary — *provided it has been previously determined that the bullet struck Governor Connally at a velocity considerably below its computed velocity for the range involved.*

The probable ballistic path and effect of a full metal-jacketed rifle bullet fired from a range of 68 yards which first passed through the President's neck and then continued on to strike Governor Connally would be essentially as follows: Starting at about 2000 feet per second (muzzle velocity), the bullet would lose approximately one third of its velocity (but not its *pristine characteristic*) reaching 68 yards and passing through the President's neck and would strike Governor Connally, point first, at a velocity of 1400-1600 feet per second. Its course through Governor Connally's chest would further reduce its velocity to 500-600 feet per second and, due to impact with the rib at reduced velocity, would lose all *pristine* characteristic, deflect slightly (probably up and to the right), and exit from the chest, wobbling (starting to wobble) on its flight axis.

The bullet then would strike the back of Governor Connally's right wrist essentially point first as it could not have turned far from point-first aspect due to the short distance (about 8 inches) and fractional time interval (about 1/800 of a second) between rib and wrist. The remaining velocity of some 500-600 feet per second would be sufficient to cause it to generate a fracture path through the wrist and continue on a probably highly deflected tumbling flight at a velocity of not more than 150 feet per second.

The bullet's termination in a shallow flesh wound in Governor Connally's left thigh, the wound indications that it struck sideways (keyholed) and at very low velocity, and its wide deflection off the line from rib to wrist, are all well within the accepted limits of ballistic variation for a full metal-jacketed bullet passing through a wrist joint at relatively low velocity.

Its high velocity transit through only the flesh of the President's neck; its medium velocity low-angle glancing impact with Governor Connally's rib; and its low velocity transit of his wrist after having lost its entire pristine characteristic; all reduce the probability of bullet deformation (of a full jacketed bullet) to a minimum.

The recovery of an only slightly deformed full metal-jacketed rifle bullet under circumstances clearly indicating that it had been on Governor Connally's person during the assassination, and the incontestable ballistic proof that it had been fired from the Mannlicher-Carcano rifle, turn. as we have observed on a previous occasion, a chain of ballistic probabilities — into a ballistic certainty.

If the foregoing were not proof enough, consider the only other alternative — that the bullet struck Governor Connally at full computed velocity. With bullet velocity increased fifty percent, the severity of his chest wound would increase twofold which, unquestionably, would have resulted in a mortal wound. His wrist would have been struck by a bullet traveling 1400-1600 feet per second. At such a velocity, a full metal-jacketed bullet would have completely shattered the wrist joint and, with only nominal deflection, if any, would have continued on its relatively high-speed course straight on towards Agent Kellerman's back with only the questionable shield of the front seat intervening.

Obviously, such a bullet track would never come close to Governor Connally's left thigh and, rather than having been recovered from Governor Connally's clothing, it would have been found imbedded in the back of the front seat — or in Agent Kellerman's back.

Governor Connally and Agent Kellerman should experience little difficulty in aligning (or unaligning) themselves with the true ballistic track of this bullet.

The Third Bullet

What became of the smaller particles of the third bullet that fragmented while transiting the President's brain case and, per the solution, shot out in various patterns in the direction of travel of the presidential limousine?

It is to be recalled that, although it was necessary to determine the paths and effects of the large sections of the third bullet recovered from the driver's compartment of the presidential limousine, our investigation did not require further tracking of the smaller fragments.

The explanations that follow will accomplish a dual purpose unintentionally — that of demonstrating the general nature of the ballistic terminations of these smaller frag-

ments and, unfortunately, that of further disparaging the
actions of the President's Commission.

Our investigation determined that only 65 grains of
this 160 grain bullet were found in the presidential limousine, so our question to be answered amounts to giving a
better accounting of the other 95 grains (by weight) of
various sized fragments which overflew the front of the
presidential limousine.

Investigative control shows us that this phenomenon
occurred at road position CPZ-313 and that the direction
of flight of these fragments, which had to overfly the
windshield of the presidential limousine, was in a fan-out
towards the Main Street tunnel of the Triple Underpass,
a distance of about 85 yards from CPZ-313.

Reference is made to an extract from the Warren Report in which the following analysis is given of "The Third
Shot — that missed." (pp. 46-47 this book, and Bant-Rep
page 111; See map plan page 186.)

. . . . . .

Mr. James T. Tague got out of his car to watch the
motorcade from a position between Commerce and Main
streets *near the Triple Underpass.* Mr. Tague testifies that
he was hit on the cheek by an object during the shooting.
He immediately reported this incident to Deputy Sheriff
Eddy R. Walthers, who immediately searched the area
where Mr. Tague had been standing and located a place
on the south curb of Main Street where it appeared a bullet
had hit the cement. In his words, "There was a mark quite
obviously that was a bullet, and it was very fresh."

The mark was scientifically examined by the FBI and
determined to be essentially lead with a trace of antimony.
By the Commission's own technical determination — the
mark on the curb could have originated from the lead

195

core of a bullet but (and here following is a preconception being applied to a misconception) the absence of copper precluded the possibility that the mark on the curbing was made by an *unmutilated* military full metal-jacketed bullet such as the bullet from Governor Connally's stretcher.

It is interesting to note that the mark was on the *south curb* of Main Street. This is significant to an investigator because it would have been highly unlikely for a fragment flying from CPZ-313 on Elm Street (which is north of Main Street) to hit the *north curb* of Main Street.

In Mr. Tague's opinion (as recorded in the Report), it was the second shot which caused the mark *since he thinks he heard the third shot after he was hit in the face.* A trained investigator quickly notes both the error in Mr. Tague's ballistic timetable — and the failure on the part of the Commission's investigators to put him straight on it. Like Mr. Holland on the railroad overpass (Triple Underpass), Mr. Tague was nearly 500 feet from the Mannlicher-Carcano rifle so the sound of the rifle report would follow the bullet (its fragments in this case) by a time lag of at least 1/3 of a second. As investigators, we would have felt called upon to question Mr. Tague's eyewitness account — if he had not heard the rifle report *after* he was struck by a fragment.

Mr. Tague's account matches the investigative control schedule and the ballistic calculations for the fragments of the third bullet exactly. Although his testimony was not required during our formal investigation, it is apparent that it corroborates and substantiates all deductions regarding the bullet which struck and killed the President at CPZ-313.

Mr. Tague, like Mr. Holland, should experience little difficulty in aligning his experiences with the solution and the ballistic facts of the case. He too, will come to realize

196

something else — how close he came to being hit and more seriously injured by a bigger fragment of the third bullet like the "core" fragment that struck and marked the south curb of Main Street very close to where he was standing.

A secondary phenomenon that was part of the multiple effect of the third bullet which struck the President did not require detailed examination or explanation during the formal investigation. As this phenomenon has been misconstrued in support of a multiple assassin theory, it will be considered here as an unanswered question.

It has to do with the movements of the President's head when he was struck by the third bullet at CPZ-313.

As correctly observed by one multiple assassin theorist, Zapruder film frames 312 through 316 ($\frac{1}{4}$ of a second of time) clearly show that the President's head moved forward perceptibly in the 1/20 of a second following his having been struck in the back of the head by the third bullet (Z-312, 313), and then made a more violent retro-movement backward and to the left in the following 3/20 of a second (Z-314, 315, and 316).

The multiple assassin theorist put together Mr. Holland's puff of smoke from the arcade area and the retro-movement of the President's head and concluded therefrom that a bullet had to be fired from the arcade area *as the only possible means* (the impact of a bullet from that direction) by which sufficient kinetic energy could be generated to cause a retro-movement of the President's head.

NOTE: A trained investigator can only shudder at seeing what can grow out of a combination of misunderstood technical factors and inadequate investigative control.

What then did cause this retro-movement?

According to the final solution as regards the third bullet to strike President Kennedy: "The impact of the third bullet caused the President's head to move forward. Instantly thereafter, the reactionary propulsive effect of the "blowout" type exit wound caused his head to move backward and to the left."

Two things are inherent in the foregoing solution. One is the ballistic certainty that the impact of a high-velocity bullet hitting squarely on the back of the President's skull caused it to move forward. The other, involving the action of an irrefutable law of physics, is the straight-line investigative determination that the "blowout" type wound resulted from "confined liquid" explosive effect which vented brain matter out through the wound orifice at high velocity which, in turn, caused the President's head to move by jet propulsion in a direction opposite to the flow of brain matter. The massive wound orifice was on the upper right side of the President's head which, at the moment of "blowout," was inclined slightly forward.

Suffice it to say that a trained and technically qualified investigator would have been seriously embarrassed — investigatively — if the President's head had not made this instantaneous propulsive retro-movement backward and to the left. Sadly enough, the only person who would have seen and physically sensed this retro-movement was Mrs. Kennedy.

Questions are bound to arise regarding the lack of notice taken of the presidential followup car and its load of eight Secret Service agents (and two presidential assistants as passengers) whose principal duty was to continuously scan the onlookers and the immediate environs and guard the President from physical harm. The followup car was almost

198

bumper to bumper behind the presidential limousine as it started down Elm Street.

The question as to why not a single one of their eyewitness accounts was used during our investigation can be answered categorically — none were needed to solve the case. From an investigator's standpoint, their testimony could have been used to solve the case, but it would have been difficult to apply it to the investigative control schedule early in the investigation. There is a technical reason for this.

As was discovered with Agent Kellerman, their jobs were to observe outward (away from the President) and, by so doing, to shield the President from any visible threat that might be observed. If threats were observed, their standing instructions were to take (or direct) such actions as would prevent harm from coming to the President.

So well laid and executed was the assassin's ambush that, as the old military instructor would put it, "they (the Secret Service agents) didn't ever know where the shots were coming from, and being in open vehicles, they had no alternative but to try to make an escape — right on down the assassin's line of fire."

The position of the followup car with respect to the presidential limousine and the assassin's firing position was such that most of the agents probably heard the "snap" of the bullets passing overhead as a composite sound with the following sound of the rifle reports.

When it is realized that these agents were confronted, in a time interval of less than 6 seconds, with the commingled sound (and echos) of three bullets "snapping" close overhead and to the right of their vehicle, and each followed or mixed with its rifle report coming from an elevated position somewhere to the rear, it is not hard to understand why their eyewitness accounts, especially as to the number and direction of the shots, varied so widely. Also, there is an object lesson here which points out why a *well-laid ambush* has so devastating an effect on a military unit.

Like Mr. Holland looking toward the arcade, these agents were desperately trying to locate the source of commingled sounds and, almost to a man, were looking away from the President when he was being hit.

There were, however, two singular exceptions — Secret Service Agent Glen A. Bennett and presidential assistant David F. Powers.

Reference is made to the Warren Report analysis of "The First Shot" . . . that missed (page 42 this book, and Bant-Rep page 108), which contains the following:

.   .   .   .   .

Some support for the contention that the first shot missed (here goes the Commission again) is found in the statement of Secret Service Agent Glen A. Bennett, stationed in the right rear seat of the presidential followup car, who heard a sound like a firecracker as the motorcade proceeded down Elm Street. At that moment (following the first firecracker sound), Agent Bennett stated: * * * I looked at the back of the President. I heard another firecracker noise and saw that shot hit the President about four inches down from the right shoulder. A second shot (actually the third) followed immediately and hit the right rear high of the President's head * * * (Warren Report continues.) Substantial weight may be given to Bennett's observations. Although his formal statement was dated November 23, 1963, his notes indicate that he recorded what he saw and heard at 5:30 P.M., November 22, 1963,

200

on the airplane enroute back to Washington, prior to the autopsy, when it was not yet known that the President had been hit in the back. It is possible, of course, (here goes the Commission again) that Bennett did not observe the hole in the President's back, which might have been there immediately after the noise (meaning after the first firecracker sound).

. . . . . .

It is certainly agreed that "substantial weight may be given Bennett's observations." His carefully recorded observations check out with the investigative control schedule and fully corroborate the final solution. The Commission's comment that Agent Bennett may have failed to see the hole in the President's back "which might have been there immediately after the noise (first shot)," clearly shows how rigidly they had locked on to the misconception that the first bullet had caused the President's neck (back) wound.

David F. Powers, Special Assistant to President Kennedy who was a passenger riding in the right hand jump seat of the presidential followup car testified as follows: (Wit-pp. 39-40)

"The first shot went off and it sounded to me as if it were a firecracker. I noticed then that the President moved quite far to his left after the shot from the extreme right hand side where he had been sitting. There was a second shot and Governor Connally disappeared from sight and then there was a third shot which took off the top of the President's head and had the sickening sound of a grapefruit splattering against the side of a wall. The total time between the first and third shots was about 5 or 6 seconds.

Author's Comment: David F. Powers proves to be an amazingly accurate observer. Even his memory of the

201

sound of a "blowout" type head wound caused by overpressure in a weakened brain case is descriptively correct. As it is a liquid rather than a gaseous explosion, it is lower-keyed than a rifle report or a firecracker explosion, but it is nevertheless a clear and distinct sound.

Had there not been the good fortune of the Zapruder film sequence upon which to establish investigative control, it is this writer's studied judgment that a satisfactory investigative control schedule could have been developed using the testimony of the two foregoing witnesses and the key witnesses riding in the presidential limousine.

Had David F. Powers been in a position to observe the *actual scalp wound* suffered by the President along with the impact effect of the first bullet which, according to him, knocked the President out of position to the left, he very probably would have solved the mystery of the bullets out of hand — on his own observations. Unfortunately, he was on the line of the lace wound rather than perpendicular to it as was Mrs. Kennedy.

His account is in perfect alignment with the investigative control schedule and matches the solution exactly.

It is very likely that other Agents in the presidential followup car will experience difficulty in aligning their impressions and memories of these few tragic seconds with events as they actually occurred. This for the same reason that would have made it difficult to fit their testimony into the investigative control schedule. Their futile efforts to locate the source of the commingled sounds directed their attentions away from, rather than towards, the presidential limousine.

The point finally has been reached where this investigation must be brought to a close. Some questions remain, but they cannot be answered here. However, with the solution at hand, the investigative control schedule within reach, and a working knowledge of good investigative procedures to go on — the author has every confidence that the reader can handle any questions that may remain — even the question, "Who was this lone assassin?"